AF454377

True Discipleship
Following Our Master to Calvary

A. W. Tozer

& Caleb Sinclair

GRAPEVINE INDIA

Published by

GRAPEVINE INDIA PUBLISHERS PVT LTD

www.grapevineindia.com
Delhi | Mumbai
email: grapevineindiapublishers@gmail.com

Ordering Information:
Quantity sales: Special discounts are available on quantity
purchases by corporations, associations, and others.
For details, reach out to the publisher.

First published by Grapevine India 2022
Copyright © Grapevine 2022

Introduction

Discipleship, obedience, surrender—these three words are almost synonymous. And there have been many profound writings on them. (Praise God!) If someone, unversed in biblical doctrine and Christian thought, picked up one of those books and flipped through it, he would wonder if all of Christendom were shamelessly promoting self-negativity.

Discipleship is by no means a comfortable topic to hear or speak about (though I would argue it is a good deal more uncomfortable for the speaker.) But it cannot be separated from the doctrine of salvation. Tozer stresses this point over and over—to receive Christ as Savior is to receive Him as Lord. To one whose spiritual eyes have been illuminated, there is no alternative.

But we today keep our feet "on both boats," and in our naivety, we think we shall be safe. A little of the world, and a little of God. Or perhaps a *lot* of the world, and a little of God too, just to be safe. The decision to draw the line at some imagined level of 'spirituality'—this much and no further—is to play with your eternal soul.

I am reminded of this quote from a film about a young Christian in Communist Russia, said by a Christian father to his son, "We can never give Him half. If we only gave Him half, it would be better in the end if we had given Him nothing at all."

Tozer emphatically teaches that this kind of half-hearted, lukewarm obedience has no place in scripture. He preached and wrote about the disciple's crucified life. A disciple hears his Master's call, and obeys at once, forsaking his fishing boat and nets.

And yet, the life of the disciple is not a painful one; it is rewarding beyond measure because it is a life lived to the fullest.

– Caleb Sinclair

1. Before Discipleship

Lost the Way

Among the many wonders of the Holy Scriptures is their ability frequently to compress into a sentence truth so vast, so complex, as to require a whole shelf of books to expound.

Even a single phrase may glow with a light like that of the ancient pillar of fire and its shining may illuminate the intellectual landscape for miles around.

An example is found in Jeremiah 10:23. The Lord had spoken of the vanity of idols and had set the glory of the living God, the King of Eternity, in contrast to the gods of the heathen. The prophet then responded in an inspired exclamation that very well states the whole problem of humankind:

"O Lord, I know that the way of man is not in himself: it is not in man that walketh to direct his steps."

The prophet here turns to a figure of speech, one which appears in the Scriptures so frequently that it is not easy to remember that it is but a figure. Man is seen as a traveler making his difficult way from a past; he can but imperfectly recollect into a future about which he knows nothing. And he cannot stay, but must each morning strike his moving tent and journey on toward.

And there is the heavy problem—toward what?

It is a simple axiom of the traveler that if he would arrive at the desired destination, he must take the right road. How far a man may have traveled is not important. What matters is whether or not he is going the right way, whether the path he is following will bring him out at the right place at last.

Sometimes there will be an end to the road, and maybe sooner than he knows. But when he has gone the last step of the way, will he find himself in a tomorrow of light and peace? Or will the day toward which he journeys be "a day of trouble and distress, a day of wasteness and desolation, a day of darkness and gloominess, a day of clouds and thick darkness"?

The inspired prophet Jeremiah says (and for that matter all the holy prophets who have spoken since the world began say) and our Lord and His apostles say that man does not know the way. Indeed, he hardly knows where he should go, to say nothing of the way he should take to get there. The worried Thomas spoke for every man when he asked, "Lord, we know not whither thou goest; and how can we know the way?"

That is the truth and we had better face it squarely: the way of man is not in himself. However severe the blow to our pride, we would do well to bow our heads and admit our ignorance. For those who know not and know that they know not, there may in the mercy of God be hope. For those who think they know, there can be only increasing darkness.

Man has lost his way philosophically. If he could think his way out of his age-old predicament, he would long ago have done it. The world has had more than enough serious-minded men of superior intellectual endowments to examine every rabbit path in all the meadows of human thought and to explore every forest and wilderness in search of the way.

Since the first fallen man got still long enough to think, fallen men have been asking these questions, "Whence came I? What am I? Why am I here? And where am I going?"

The noblest minds of the race have struggled with these questions to no avail. If the answer did lie somewhere hidden like a jewel, it would surely have been uncovered, for the most penetrating minds of the race have searched for it. Not a foot of ground but has been spaded up, neither is there crevice or cave anywhere in the region of human experience that has not spied into thoroughly and often as the centuries passed. Yet the answers remain as securely hidden as if they did not exist.

Why is man lost philosophically? Because he is lost morally and spiritually. He cannot answer the questions life presents to his intellect because the light of God has gone out in his soul. The fearful indictment the Holy Ghost brings against mankind is summed up count by count in the opening chapters of Romans, and the conduct of every man from earliest recorded history to the present moment is evidence enough to sustain the indictment.

"When they knew God, they glorified him not as God," read the terrible words, *"neither were thankful; but became vain in their imaginations, and their foolish heart was darkened. Professing themselves to be wise, they became fools, and changed the glory of the uncorruptible God into an image made like to corruptible man, and to birds, and four-footed beasts, and creeping things… who changed the truth of God into a lie."*

On and on the devastating words flow, mounting in intensity till no one with any conscience left or any fear of moral consequences can stand to look the Judge in the face, but must cast down his guilty eyes and cry, "Have mercy upon me, O God, according to thy loving-kindness: according to the multitude of thy tender mercies blot out my transgressions."

Apart from the Scriptures we have no sure philosophy; apart from Jesus Christ we have no true knowledge of God; apart from the inliving Spirit we have no ability to live lives morally pleasing to God.

How wonderful that Christ could say, "I am the way, the truth, and the life." For this we can never be thankful enough.

Obstructions to Intimacy

Intimacy with the Creator separates man from all other of God's creation. The great passion buried in the breast of every human being created in the image of God is to experience this awesome majesty of His presence. However, several things stand in the way of man's striving toward the presence of God in personal, intimate familiarity.

The experience of too many people trying to probe the presence of God ends in complete and utter frustration. Longing to be in His presence and actually coming into His presence are two entirely different things. As created beings, man longs for the presence of the Creator, but in himself cannot find it.

Consider the eagle, born to fly. A natural yearning within the breast of the young eagle leads it to mount up on wings and ascend into the sky with a thousand feet of clean air beneath its wings. The eagle may, on occasion, walk on the ground or perch in a tree, but everything about him is designed to fly in the air. If our eagle had its wings clipped, preventing him from flying, he still would have the burning desire to mount up on wings and ascend into the sky. His ability, however, would be so impaired that he could never lift off the ground. He could not be true to his nature.

Such is the plight of humanity. We are born to ascend into the very environment of God's presence where we belong; but something has clipped our wings, disabling us from responding to the cry from within. *"Deep calleth unto deep at the noise of thy waterspouts: all thy waves and thy billows are gone over me."* (Ps. 42:7)

Because man is shut out of the presence of God, he suffers many maladies. The greatest hindrance, of course, is the fact that God is unapproachable. Sin has created an unmanageable debt for all humanity. The good news, however, is that Christ has paid the debt and bridged that gap to God for all. But there are still at least three challenges that stand in man's way as he strives after God's presence.

The first obstruction is the *moral bankruptcy of the human soul*. Man's inevitable striking against the kingdom of God and the moral order of the universe puts him in debt to that moral order, and becomes a debt to the great God who created the heavens and earth. This debt must be paid. The moral conscience of all men requires and cries out for a fund of merit sufficient to pay that debt.

That's why every religion tries to establish this fund of merit—but without success. Religion does it through what is referred to as "good works," resulting in emptiness and a deep-seated sense of guilt that nothing can wash away. But even if such a fund of merit could be achieved, it would not be enough. Pardon must be secured.

Secondly, man cannot enter the presence of God with the *foul scent of sin* upon him. Although the past has been dealt with, the present condition also must be addressed. The very presence of sinful thoughts, for example, inhibits our approach into the presence of God. The filth clinging to our robe of self-righteousness repulses the pure, undefiled presence of God. Not only do we need a change of heart, but we also need a change of garment. Therefore, we must exchange our filthy garment for the pure robe of righteousness. To come into the presence of God, we must conform in every way to His standard.

In light of this standard, some provision must be made available. Some fountain must be opened in the House of David for sin and uncleanness so that we may not only be forgiven but also cleansed.

The blood of Jesus Christ accomplished this stupendous act! This is what Christianity teaches. This is the witness the Church gives to the world. Man's moral conscience, crying for pardon and cleansing before the presence of the great God, has now found it by an event, an act of the eternal Son, who is the image of the invisible God and the firstborn of every creature, upholding all things by the Word of His power (see Col. 1:15-17). He turned aside to do this awful act—this awesome, amazing, stupendous act—by Himself. He single-handedly purged our sins. He alone could do it, so He did it alone.

The present generation of Christians has also suffered what I call the *lost concept of majesty*. This has come about by a slow decline, manifesting itself in our depreciation of ourselves. Those who hold a low value of man have a corresponding low value of God. After all, God created man in His own image. When we cease to understand the majestic nature of man, we cease to appreciate the majesty of God. Even Christians suffer with a demoralized sense of majesty. It does not matter whether it is true or not as long as it is funny. We do not care whether it is truth or not if it is said in a cute way that entertains us.

But I believe the Majesty is still in the heavens. This Majesty still sits on His throne before which angels, archangels, seraphim and cherubim continue to cry, "Holy, holy, holy, Lord God of Sabbaoth." When Jesus, who was God by Himself, alone purged our sins, He went back and sat down where He had been through the long, long ages—at the right hand of the Majesty in the heavens. After He sat down on that right hand, the eternal Son turned to man.

Jesus' Teachings Are for The Church

A generation or so ago when Modernism was rising in religious circles, a great deal was heard about the ethics of Jesus and the tragic failure of the Church to get those ethics accepted by society.

The assumption was that our Lord had introduced into the world a superior system of ethics, based upon love and leading to brotherhood, and that His plan was to spread this new doctrine through the agency of the Church till throughout the whole wide world men "should brothers be, for a' that and a' that."

It may seem a bit odd that the religious teachers who exalted the teachings of Jesus to the seventh empyrean should in the same breath demote the person of Jesus to the level of a common man; yet they did just that.

They lamented with many a crocodile tear the error of the Church in worshiping Jesus and failing to spread His ethics throughout the earth. The implication was that the man Jesus was important only because of the sterling quality of His ethics; though it was hard for some then and it is hard for others now to understand how a man's teaching can be greater than the man. The same persons who exalted His doctrine of love completely ignored His claim to deity, and brushed aside His teachings on sin, judgment, and hell, as well as His whole system of eschatology.

This arrogant picking and choosing among the words of Christ gave some persons the impression that these teachers were far less sincere than they claimed to be. For a man need not be a genius to reach the conclusion that if Jesus was wrong about almost all of His teachings, there could be no certainty that He was right about the rest.

Well, it is not my intention to fight again the battle of Bunker Hill. If all this belonged only to the past, we might be content to let the dead bury their dead and pass on to something else. But the ghosts of the old Modernists appear to have been reincarnated, and many of the arguments raised by the liberals a generation ago are now being repeated by the orthodox.

The ethics of Jesus must be imposed upon society, we are told, for then all inequalities will vanish. The division of humanity into rich and poor, great and small, privileged and underprivileged will be no more. Under the benign influence of Christ's ethics of love, greed and war will disappear from the earth and the dream of universal brotherhood be realized at last.

Back of such teachings lie several grave errors, possibly the worst being the failure to distinguish the Church of Christ from the fallen world of mankind. According to the Bible the human race is morally fallen, spiritually alienated from God, lost and under the severe sentence of divine judgment.

In sharp contrast to this, the Church is a body of regenerated persons who have withdrawn from the world in spirit and in heart and have thrown in their lot with Christ to own Him as Savior and to follow Him as Lord.

Between these two groups, the world and the Church, there is a gulf as wide as space. The truly regenerated man is a new creature; he belongs to another order of being; he has another kind of life, another origin, another destiny. He is like those who sailed in the ark of Noah touching the watery world of lost men, to be sure, but separated from it by a thin hull that might as well have been miles thick, for it kept them in and kept the judgment water out.

The teachings of Jesus belong to the Church, not to society. In society is sin, and sin is hostility to God. Christ did not teach that He would impose His teachings upon the fallen world. He called His disciples to Him and taught them, and everywhere throughout His teachings there is the overt or implied idea that His followers will constitute an unpopular minority group in an actively hostile world.

The divine procedure is to go into the world of fallen men, preach to them the necessity to repent and become disciples of Christ and, after making disciples, to teach them the "ethics of Jesus," which Christ called "all things whatsoever I have commanded you."

The ethics of Jesus cannot be obeyed or even understood until the life of God has come to the heart of a man in the miracle of the new birth. The righteousness of the law is fulfilled in them who walk in the Spirit. Christ lives again in His redeemed follower the life He lived in Judaea; for righteousness can never be divorced from its source, which is Jesus Christ Himself.

The dream of a universal brotherhood based upon the ethics of Jesus is just that—a dream. It is compounded of a few words of Christ mixed with vast numbers of uninspired words spoken by men whose yearnings are to be commended but whose wisdom is suspect. To arrive at the doctrine of brotherhood it is necessary that we reject the major portion of the New Testament and misunderstand the rest.

There were once two brothers. They lived in a society that had not had time to develop the many social evils we know today. Yet one killed the other because sin was there. If two brothers in the morning of the world could not get on together, how can we hope that the gentle teachings of Jesus can ever bring brotherhood to a race filled with complex iniquities, where men inherit hates and where the souls of all are lacerated by jealousy, envy, egotism, greed and lust?

The hope of the individual is the new birth and the acceptance of the teachings of Christ as a way of life. The hope of the race is that Christ shall come again to earth. Even so, Lord, come quickly.

An Inclusive Invitation

It is like the Lord to fasten a world upon nothing, and make it stay in place. Here He takes that wonderful, mysterious microcosm we call the human soul and makes its future weal or woe to rest upon a single word— "if."

"If any man," He says, and teaches at once the universal inclusiveness of His invitation, and the freedom of the human will. Everyone may come; no one need come. And whoever does come, comes because he chooses to.

Every man holds his future in his hand. Not only the dominant world leader, but even the inarticulate man lost in anonymity is a "man of destiny." He decides which way his soul shall go. He chooses, and destiny waits on the nod of his head. He decides, and either hell enlarges herself, or heaven prepares another mansion. So much of Himself has God given to men.

There is a strange beauty in the ways of God with men. He sends salvation to the world in the person of a Man, and sends that Man to walk the busy ways saying, "If any man will come after me."

No drama, no fanfare, no tramp of marching feet or tumult of shouting. A kindly Stranger walks through the earth, and so quiet is His voice that it is sometimes lost in the hurly-burly; but it is the last voice of God, and until we become quiet to hear it we have no authentic message. He bears good tidings from afar but He compels no man to listen. "If any man will," He says, and passes on.

Friendly, courteous, unobtrusive, He yet bears the signet of the King. His word is divine authority, His eyes a tribunal, His face a last judgment.

"If any man will… let him follow me," He says, and some will rise and go after Him, but others give no heed to His voice.

So the gulf opens between man and man, between those who will and those who will not. Silently, terribly the work goes on, as each one decides whether he will hear or ignore the voice of invitation. Unknown to the world, perhaps unknown even to the individual, the work of separation takes place.

Each hearer of the Voice must decide for himself, and he must decide on the basis of the evidence the message affords. There will be no thunder sound, no heavenly sign or light from heaven. The Man is His own proof. The marks in His hands and feet are the insignia of His rank and office. He will not put Himself again on trial; He will not argue, but the morning of the judgment will confirm what men in the twilight have decided.

And those who would follow Him must accept His conditions. "Let him," He says, and there is no appeal from His words. He will use no coercion, but neither will He compromise. Men cannot make the terms; they merely agree to them. Thousands turn from Him because they will not meet His conditions. He watches them as they go, for He loves them, but He will make no concessions. Admit one soul into the Kingdom by compromise, and that Kingdom is no longer secure. Christ will be Lord, or He will be Judge. Every man must decide whether he will take Him as Lord now or face Him as Judge then.

What are the terms of discipleship? Only one with a perfect knowledge of mankind could have dared to make them. Only the Lord of men could have risked the effect of such rigorous demands: "Let him deny himself."

We hear these words and shake our heads in astonishment. Can we have heard aright? Can the Lord lay down such severe rules at the door of the Kingdom?

He can and He does. If He is to save the man, He must save him from himself. It is the "himself" which has enslaved and corrupted the man. Deliverance comes only by denial of that self. No man in his own strength can shed the chains with which self has bound him, but in the next breath the Lord reveals the source of the power which is to set the soul free: "Let him take up his cross."

The cross has gathered in the course of the years much of beauty and symbolism, but the cross of which Jesus spoke had nothing of beauty in it. It was an instrument of death. Slaying men was its only function. Men did not wear that cross; but that cross wore men. It stood naked until a man was pinned on it, a living man fastened like some grotesque stickpin on its breast to writhe and groan till death stilled and silenced him. That is the cross. Nothing less. And when it is robbed of its tears and blood and pain, it is the cross no longer.

"Let him take ... his cross," said Jesus, and in death he will know deliverance from himself.

A strange thing under the sun is cross-less Christianity. The cross of Christendom is a no-cross, an ecclesiastical symbol. The cross of Christ is a place of death. Let each one be careful which cross he carries.

"And follow me." Now the glory begins to break in upon the soul that has just returned from Calvary. "Follow me" is an invitation, and a challenge, and a promise. The cross has been the end of a life and the beginning of a life. The life that ended there was a life of sin and slavery; the life that began there is a life of holiness and spiritual freedom.

"And follow me," He says, and faith runs on tiptoe to keep pace with the advancing light. Until we know the program of our risen Lord for all the years to come, we can never know everything He meant when He invited us to follow Him. Each heart can have its own dream of fair worlds and new revelations, of the odyssey of the ransomed soul in the ages to come, but whoever follows Jesus will find at last that He has made the reality to outrun the dream.

2. The Terms of Discipleship – Death and Denial

If any man will come after me, let him deny himself, and take up his cross, and follow me.

MATTHEW 16:24

'Accepting' Christ

Some things in our human lives are so basically unimportant that we never miss them if we do not have them. Some other things, even some that we just take for granted, are so important that if we do not grasp them and hold them and secure them for all eternity, we will suffer irreparable loss and anguish.

When we come to the question of our own relationship with God through the merits of our Lord Jesus Christ, we come to one of those areas that in a supreme degree is truly a matter of life and death.

This is so desperately a matter of importance for every human being who comes into the world that I first become indignant, and then I become sad, when I try to give spiritual counsel to a person who looks me in the eye and tells me, "Well, I am trying to make up my mind if I should accept Christ or not." Such a person gives absolutely no indication that he realizes he is talking about the most important decision he can make in his lifetime—a decision to get right with God, to believe in the eternal Son, the Savior, to become a disciple, an obedient witness to Jesus Christ as Lord.

How can any man or woman, lost and undone, sinful and wretched, alienated from God, stand there and intimate that the death and resurrection of Jesus Christ and God's revealed plan of salvation do not take priority over some of life's other decisions?

Now, the particular attitude revealed here about "accepting Christ" is wrong because it makes Christ stand hat-in-hand, somewhere outside the door, waiting on our human judgment.

We know about His divine person. We know that He is the Lamb of God who suffered and died in our place. We know all about His credentials. Yet we let Him stand outside on the steps like some poor timid fellow who is hoping he can find a job. We look Him over, then read a few more devotional verses, and ask: "What do you think, Mabel? Do you think we ought to accept Him? I really wonder if we should accept Him."

And so, in this view, our poor Lord Christ stands hat-in-hand, shifting from one foot to another looking for a job, wondering whether He will be accepted. Meanwhile, there sits the proud Adamic sinner, rotten as the devil and filled with all manner of spiritual leprosy and cancer. But he is hesitating; he is judging whether or not he will accept Christ.

Doesn't that proud human know that the Christ he is putting off is the Christ of God, the eternal Son who holds the worlds in His hands? Does he not know that Christ is the eternal Word, the Jesus who made the heavens and the earth and all things that are therein? Why, this One who patiently waits for our human judgment is the One who holds the stars in His hands. He is the Savior and Lord and head over all things to the church. It will be at His word that the graves shall give up their dead, and the dead shall come forth, alive forevermore. At His word, the fire shall burst loose and burn up the earth and the heavens and the stars and planets shall be swept away like a garment.

He is the One, the Mighty One! And yet there He stands, while we animated clothespins—that's what we look like and that's what we are—decide whether we will accept Him or not. How grotesque can it be? The question ought not to be whether I will accept Him; the question ought to be whether He will accept me!

But He does not make that a question. He has already told us that we do not have to worry or disturb our minds about that. *"And him that cometh to me I will in no wise cast out."* (John 6:37)

He has promised to receive us, poor and sinful though we be. But the idea that we can make Him stand while we render the verdict of whether He is worthy of our acceptance is a frightful calumny—and we ought to get rid of it!

Now, I think we should get back to our original premise that our relationship to Jesus Christ is a matter of life or death to us. The average person with even a minimum of instruction in church or Sunday school will generally take two things for granted, without argument. The first is that Jesus Christ came into the world to save sinners. That is declared specifically in the Bible, and it is declared in other words adding up to the same thing all through the New Testament. If we have been reared in gospel churches, we also generally will take for granted the second fact: that we are saved by faith in Christ alone, without our works and without our merit.

A Saving Relationship

I am discussing these two basic things with you here because too many individuals take them for granted, believe them to be true; and still they are asking, "How do I know that I have come into a saving relationship with Jesus Christ?" We had better find the answer because this is the matter of life or death.

The fact that Christ Jesus came into the world to save sinners is a matter of record. It needs no further proof. It is a fact—yet the world is not saved! Right here in America, in our own neighborhoods, thousands and tens of thousands of people still are not saved. Just the fact that He came to save sinners is not enough—that fact in itself cannot save us.

A friend or neighbor may tell us, "Well, I have gone to this certain church all my life. I have been confirmed, baptized and all the rest. I am going to take the chance that it will get me through."

My friend, your odds are not that good—you do not even have a chance. If your relation to Jesus Christ is not a saving relation, then you are on your own without a guide and without a compass. It is not a chance you have; it is suicide that you are committing. It is not a chance in ten times ten thousand. It is either be right or be dead; in this case, be right or be eternally lost.

There are millions all around us who have some Bible knowledge. They would tell you they have no argument with the fact that Jesus Christ came into the world to save sinners. They may even make a little joke about their own failures and shortcomings—they would not call them sins. They would likely excuse themselves from having to make a personal decision because they are not nearly as bad as Mr. Jones or Mrs. Smith down the street.

The point is that they may be able to recite John 3:16 or quote something nice about the whole world needing a Savior—and in an unusually tender moment there might be the sign of a tear in the eye. But they are lost. They are really far from God. They know that they are not converted because they have all known some person who had confessed Jesus Christ, been soundly converted and started living a transformed life.

Yes, they all know the difference. They know they are not converted, but they would rather not be told about the fate of the sinner when he dies. Oh, that lost men and women would get concerned to the point of asking and finding out how they may come into a saving relationship with the Savior, Jesus Christ!

Now, go to the average Christian brother, a converted man and probably a substitute teacher for the Bible class, and ask him: "How can I come into a saving relation to Jesus Christ so that it works for me?"

He will probably give you one of three answers, or he may give you all three answers. If you came to me, you would get the same, so this is not a criticism of anyone. This is simply a statement. You would get the same answer from Billy Graham and you would get the same answer from the most isolated and unknown layman who has committed his way to Jesus Christ.

First, you would be told that it is a matter of faith, that you must believe what God says about His Son, as in Acts 16:31: *"Believe on the Lord Jesus Christ, and thou shalt be saved."* That is the Bible answer that you would get.

Then, the person answering your question might add: "There is also the willingness to receive from God, as in John 1:12: *'But as many as received him ... even to them that believe on his name.'"* So there in John's gospel, you find the close relationship in faith of believing and receiving.

But in our day, you will also be likely to get a third answer, and that is the one we are considering here. In all likelihood, if you would ask a number of Christian people how to come into this blessed saving relationship with Christ, someone is going to tell you: "Why, you just accept Christ!"

Let me say here that I do not want to make God responsible for anything I do, or anything I tell you. I have had my long talks with God and He knows how grateful and thankful I am if He can bless me and guide me and use me to do a few little things for Him. He surely knows that I am available as long as I am able to pray and think and speak a good word for Him, as long as I last.

What I am saying on this contemporary subject of "accepting Christ" is not a personal whim. Actually, I was kneeling by the little couch in my study upstairs, kneeling there with my Bible open, and I was engaged with God in doing a little repenting on my own accord—my own.

All of this came to me so clearly that I just wrote down a few notes, and said, "I am going to talk to the people about this." You are my friends, and I tell you that perhaps I am introducing some things here that God did not say to me, but maybe you will agree that you would rather hear a sermon from the outline the man got while on his knees than to know that he had gotten it somewhere else.

Well, that is it; a popular answer in our day is that we find Christ by accepting Him. You will find when I am through that I am not being critical. Probably our expressions in language do not always tell us what our hearts know.

Easy Acceptance Is Fatal

You may be surprised, as I was, when I ran this thing down and found that the expression "accept Christ" does not occur in the Bible. It is not found in the New Testament at all.

I have looked it up in *Strong's Exhaustive Concordance*, and the old editors worked on that volume so long and so thoroughly that it does not skip a single word. Strong's concordance shows very definitely that the word accept is never used in the Bible in the sense of our accepting God or accepting Jesus as our Savior.

It does seem strange that while we do not find its use anywhere in the Bible, the phrase, "Will you accept Christ?" or "Have you accepted Christ?" have become the catchwords throughout our soul-winning circles. I am not trying to question our good intentions. I am sure that I have used this same expression many times—but still we have to admit that it does not occur in the Bible at all.

The words *accept* and *acceptance* are used in the Scriptures in a number of ways, but never in connection with believing on Christ or receiving Christ for salvation or being saved. My concern in this matter is my feeling that "easy acceptance" has been fatal to millions of people who may have stopped short in matters of faith and obedience.

It is interesting to note that many groups of Christian workers and preachers and evangelists everywhere are calling for revival. Spiritual life in many areas seems to be in a low state, and in many cases, people are passing along the word about "prayer for revival." But here is the odd thing: no one seems to stop and raise a question, such as: "Perhaps the reason we need revival so badly is the fact that we did not get started right in the first place." This is why I have questioned the wide use of the soul-winning catchword, "Will you accept Christ? Just bow your head and accept Christ!"

I cannot estimate the number, although I think it is a very large number, of people who have been brought into some kind of religious experience by a fleeting formality of "accepting Christ," and a great, great number of them are still not saved. They have not been brought into a genuine saving relationship with Jesus Christ. We see the results all around us—they generally behave like religious sinners instead of like born-again believers.

That is why there is such a great stirring about the need for revival. That is why so many are asking, "What is the matter with us? We seem so dead, so lifeless, so apathetic about spiritual things!"

I say again that I have come to the conclusion that there are far too many among us who have thought that they accepted Christ—but nothing has come of it within their own lives and desires and habits. Will you just examine this matter a little more closely with me?

This kind of philosophy in soul winning, the idea that it is the easiest thing in the world to "accept Jesus," permits the man or woman to accept Christ by an impulse of the mind or emotions. It allows us to gulp twice and sense an emotional feeling that may come over us, and then say, "I have accepted Christ."

All of you are aware of some of the very evident examples of the shortcomings in this approach to conversion and the new birth. A Christian lady interested in the boys and girls goes out to the playground where several hundred children are engaged in their play and games. When she comes back, she reports with enthusiasm that she was able to persuade a group of about seventy children to stop their play and "accept Christ in their hearts."

I actually was told of a group of preachers and laymen gathered in a hotel dining room and when the issue of soul-winning came up, one of the preachers said, "It is the easiest thing in the world, and I will give you a demonstration."

When the waiter came to his table, this brother said, "Can I have a minute of your time?"

The waiter said, "Yes, sir."

"Are you a Christian?" the preacher asked.

"No, sir. I am not a Christian."

"Wouldn't you like to be a Christian?"

"Well—well, I haven't thought too much about it."

"You know, all you have to do is accept Christ into your heart—will you accept Him?"

"Well, I guess so—yes, sir."

"All right, then, you just bow your head for a moment."

So, while the man who has been placed in a corner is thinking most about his tip, the soul-winner prays: "Now, Lord, here is a man who wants to accept You. And he takes You now as his Savior. Bless him real good. Amen!"

So, the waiter gets an enthusiastic handshake, and turns away to do his job, and he is just the same as when he came into the room.

But the demonstrating preacher turns to the group and says, "It is a simple matter. You can all see how easy it is to lead someone to Christ."

I think these are matters about which we must be legitimately honest and in which we must seek the discernment of the Holy Spirit. I hope that the waiter had better sense than the reverend, because he is damned if he did not.

These are things about which we cannot afford to be wrong. To be wrong is to still be lost and far from God. This is a matter of life or death and eternity. When we are considering the importance to any human being of a right and saving relationship to Jesus Christ, we cannot afford to be wrong.

I think there is much abuse and that it is a great misconception to try to deal with men and women in this shallow manner when we know the great importance of conviction and concern and repentance when it comes to conversion, spiritual regeneration, being born from above by the Spirit of God. It would be a healthy sign if the whole church of Christ would rise up and ask God for fresh air in this matter; asking God for courage to consider and analyze where we stand in our efforts to win people to the Savior.

I am not trying to downgrade anybody in his or her efforts to win souls. I am just of the opinion that we are often too casual and there are too many tricks that can be used to make soul-winning encounters completely painless and at no cost and with no inconvenience.

Some people that we deal with on this "quick and easy" basis have such little preparation and are so ignorant of the plan of salvation that they would be willing to bow their heads and "accept" Buddha or Zoroaster or Father Divine if they thought that they could get rid of us in that way.

I think back to that time when God was dealing with the Israelites in bondage in Egypt. Suppose that Moses had said to the Israelites, "Do you accept the blood on the doorpost?"

They would have said, "Yes, of course. We accept the blood."

Moses then would have said, "That's fine. Now goodbye; I will be seeing you."

They would have stayed right in Egypt, slaves for the rest of their lives. But their acceptance of the blood was a decision of action. Their acceptance of the blood of the Passover meant that they stayed awake all night; girded, ready, shoes on their feet, staffs in their hands, eating the food of the Passover, ready for the moving of God.

Then, when the trumpet blasts sang sweet and clear, they all arose and started for the Red Sea. When they got to the Red Sea, having acted in faith, God was there to hold back the sea and they went out, never to return! Their acceptance had the right kind of feet under it. Their acceptance gave them the guts to do something about it in the demonstration of their faith in God and His word.

Consider also the case of the prodigal son in the midst of the pigs with their dirt and filth and smell. Suppose you were concerned about him, about his own rags and his hunger.

"I have good news for you," you tell him. "Your father will forgive you if you will accept it. Will you accept it?"

He looks up from where he is reclining among the pigs, trying to keep warm, and replies: "Yeah, I'll accept it."

"Do you accept your father's reconciling and saving word?"

"Yes, I do!"

"That's fine. All right, goodbye. Hope to see you again."

You leave him in the pigpen. You leave him still in the dirt and filth. But that is not the way it happened in the story Jesus told in Luke 15.

The fellow was in there with the pigs and the filth—but something was stirring in his own heart and mind, and he said within himself: "If I am ever going to get out of this mess, I will have to make a decision. I must arise and go to my father."

I guess all of us know the next line:

"So he got up and went!"

Remember that?

"So he got up and went!"

Acceptance to the Jews meant strict obedience from that moment on. Acceptance to the prodigal son meant repentance in line with his acceptance.

I realize that the word *accept* has come close to being a synonym for the word receive. But I want to tell you what it means to accept Christ and then I want you to search your own heart and say, "Have I ever really accepted Christ? Do I accept Christ? Have I accepted Him at all?"

Exclusive Attachment That Transforms

I want to give you a definition for accepting Christ.

To accept Christ in anything like a saving relation is to have an attachment to the person of Christ that is revolutionary, complete, and exclusive.

What I am talking about is an attachment to the person of Christ, and that is so important. It is something more than getting in with a crowd that you like. It is something more than the social fellowship of some nice fellow that gives you a thrill when you touch his hand. It is something more than getting in with a group that puts on their uniforms and plays softball together on Tuesday evenings.

Those things are all harmless enough, God knows. But accepting Jesus Christ is more than finding association with a group you like. It is not just going on a picnic or taking a hike. We have those activities in our church and I believe in them. But they are not the things that are as important as your acceptance of Jesus Christ. The answer you are seeking in Jesus Christ does not mean that you are just getting in with a religious group who may not be any better off than you are.

Accepting Jesus Christ, receiving Jesus Christ into your life means that you have made an attachment to the person of Christ that is revolutionary in that it reverses the life and transforms it completely. It is an attachment to the person of Christ. It is complete in that it leaves no part of the life unaffected. It exempts no area of the life of the total man; his total being.

This kind of an attachment to the person of Christ means that Christ is not just one of several interests. It means that He is the one exclusive attachment as the sun is the exclusive attachment of the earth. As the earth revolves around the sun, and the sun is its center and the core of its being, so Jesus Christ is the Son of righteousness, and to become a Christian by the grace of God means to come into His orbit and begin to revolve around Him exclusively.

In the sense of spiritual life and desire and devotion, it means to revolve around Him completely, exclusively—not partly around Him.

This does not mean that we do not have other relationships—we all do because we all live in a complex world. You give your heart to Jesus. He becomes the center of your transformed life. But you may be a man with a family. You are a citizen of the country. You have a job and an employer. In the very nature of things, you have other relationships.

But by faith and through grace, you have now formed an exclusive relationship with your Savior, Jesus Christ. All of your other relationships are now conditioned and determined by your one relationship to Jesus Christ, the Lord.

Jesus laid down the terms of Christian discipleship and there have been people who have criticized and said, "Those words of Jesus sound harsh and cruel." His words were plain and He was saying to every one of us: "If you have other relationships in life which are more important and more exclusive than your spiritual relationship to the eternal Savior, then you are not My disciple."

To accept Christ, then, is to attach ourselves to His holy person; to live or die, forever. He must be first and last and all. All of our other relationships are conditioned and determined and colored by our one exclusive relation to Him. To accept Christ without reservation is to accept His friends as your friends from that moment on.

If you find yourself in an area where Christ has no friends, you will be friendless except for the one Friend who sticketh closer than a brother. It means that you will not compromise your life. You will neither compromise your talk nor your habits of life.

We have to confess that we find there are people who are such cowards that when they are with a crowd that denies the Son of God and disgraces the holy name of Jesus, they allow themselves to be carried away in that direction. Are they Christians? You will have to answer that.

A Christian is one who has accepted Jesus' friends as his friends and Jesus' enemies as his enemies by an exclusive attachment to the person of Christ.

I made up my mind a long time ago. Those who declare themselves enemies of Jesus Christ must look upon me as their enemy—and I ask no quarter from them. And if they are the friends of Jesus Christ, they are my friends and I do not care what color they are or what denomination they belong to.

To accept the Lord means to accept His ways as our ways. We have taken His Word and His teachings as the guide in our lives. To accept Christ means that I accept His rejection as my rejection. When I accept Him, I knowingly and willingly accept His cross as my cross. I accept His life as my life—back from the dead I come and up into a different kind of life. It means that I accept His future as my future.

I am talking about the necessity of an exclusive attachment to His person—that is what it means to accept Christ. If the preachers would tell people what it actually means to accept Christ and receive Him and obey Him and live for Him, we would have fewer converts, but those who would come and commit would not backslide and founder. They would stick.

Actually, preachers and ministers of the gospel of Christ should remember that they are going to stand before the judgment seat of Christ, and they will have to tell a holy Savior why they betrayed His people in this way.

Now, please do not go out and tell people that Mr. Tozer says you should never use those words, "accept Christ." I have tried to make it plain that we should always invite those who are not Christians to come to Jesus, to believe what God says about the Savior, to receive Him by faith into their lives and to obey Him; and to accept Christ as their Savior if they know what it means—an exclusive attachment to the person of Christ.

3. The Rock of the Disciple

To show that the LORD is upright: he is my rock, and there is no unrighteousness in him.

PSALM 92:15

A God Who Loves

God, being who and what He is, must love Himself with pure and perfect love.

The Persons of the Godhead love each other with a love so fiery, so tender, that it is all a burning flame of intense desire ineffable.

God is Himself the only being whom He can love directly; all else that He loves is for His own sake and because He finds some reflection of Himself there.

God loves His mute creation because He sees in it an imperfect representation of His own wisdom and power. He loves the angels and seraphim because He sees in them some likeness of His holiness. He loves men because He beholds in them a fallen relic of His own image.

Potentially God loves all men alike, but His active love lights upon some men more than upon others, the degree depending upon how much of Himself He is able to impart to them. The truly Christlike soul enjoys more of God's love because God sees in it a truer image of Himself than in a soul less purified. God loves His Son with infinite perfection because He is "the brightness of his glory, and the express image of his person."

God desires that all men should become Christlike, for in so doing they present larger and more perfect objects for the reception of His outpoured love.

Conformity to the nature of Christ on the part of a redeemed man restores the image of God in the soul, and thus makes it possible for God to lavish on the soul without restraint all the boundless love of which He is the original fountain.

It is hard for a sinful man to believe that God loves Him. His own accusing conscience tells him it could not be so. He knows that he is an enemy of God and alienated in his mind through wicked works, and he sees in himself a thousand moral discrepancies that unfit him for the just enjoyment of so pure a love.

Yet the whole Bible proclaims the love of God for sinful men. We must believe in His love because He declares it and avail ourselves of the sanctifying grace of Christ in order to receive and enjoy that love to the full.

"For our soul is so specially loved of Him that is highest, that it over-passeth the knowing of all creatures ... there is no creature that is made that may fully know how much and how sweetly and how ten-derly our Maker loveth us. And therefore we may with grace and His help (behold) with everlasting marvel this high, overpassing, in-estimable love that Almighty God hath to us of His goodness. And therefore we may ask of our Lover with reverence all that we will."

God is love, and is for that reason the source of all the love there is. He has set as the first of all commandments that we love Him with all our hearts, but He knows that the desired love can never originate with us. "We love him, because he first loved us," is the scriptural and psychological pattern. We can love Him as we ought only as He inflames our minds with holy desire.

Yet there is also a love of willing as well as of feeling. Though we may not be conscious of any great degree of inward sensation, we may set our wills to love God and the feeling will come of itself. Let us bring ourselves under obedience to His revealed Word and our love for Him will grow. Obedience will strengthen faith and faith will increase knowledge.

And it is a well-known law of the spiritual life that our love for God will spring up and flourish just as our knowledge of Him increases. To know Him is to love Him, and to know Him better is to love Him more.

A Winsome God

Satan's first attack upon the human race was his sly effort to destroy Eve's confidence in the kindness of God. Unfortunately for her and for us, he succeeded too well. From that day, men have had a false conception of God, and it is exactly this that has cut out from under them the ground of righteousness and driven them to reckless and destructive living.

Nothing twists and deforms the soul more than a low or unworthy conception of God. Certain sects, such as the Pharisees, while they held that God was stern and austere, yet managed to maintain a fairly high level of external morality; but their righteousness was only outward. Inwardly they were "whited sepulchres," as our Lord Himself told them (Matthew 23:27).

Their wrong conception of God resulted in a wrong idea of worship. To a Pharisee, the service of God was a bondage which he did not love, but from which he could not escape without a loss too great to bear. The God of the Pharisee was not a God easy to live with, so his religion became grim and hard and loveless. It had to be so, for our notion of God must always determine the quality of our religion.

Much Christianity since the days of Christ's flesh has also been grim and severe. And the cause has been the same—an unworthy or an inadequate view of God. Instinctively we try to be like our God, and if He is conceived to be stern and exacting, so will we ourselves be.

From a failure properly to understand God comes a world of unhappiness among good Christians even today. The Christian life is thought to be a glum, unrelieved cross-carrying life under the eye of a stern Father who expects much and excuses nothing. He is austere, peevish, highly temperamental and extremely hard to please. The kind of life which springs out of such libelous notions must of necessity be but a parody on the true life in Christ.

It is most important to our spiritual welfare that we always hold in our minds a right conception of God. If we think of Him as cold and exacting, we shall find it impossible to love Him, and our lives will be ridden with servile fear. If, again, we hold Him to be kind and understanding, our whole inner life will mirror that idea.

The truth is that God is the most winsome of all beings, and His service one of unspeakable pleasure. He is all love, and those who trust Him need never know anything but that love. He is just indeed, and He will not condone sin; but through the blood of the everlasting covenant, He is able to act toward us exactly as if we had never sinned. Toward the trusting sons of men His mercy will always triumph over justice.

The fellowship of God is delightful beyond all telling. He communes with His redeemed ones in an easy, uninhibited fellowship that is restful and healing to the soul. He is not sensitive or selfish nor temperamental. What He is today we shall find Him tomorrow and the next day and the next year.

He is not hard to please, though He may be hard to satisfy. He expects of us only what He has Himself first supplied. He is quick to mark every simple effort to please Him, and just as quick to overlook imperfections when He knows we meant to do His will. He loves us for ourselves and values our love more than galaxies of new created worlds.

And when it comes to redemption, this was not a heavy task laid upon God by moral necessity. God wanted to do this. There was no moral necessity upon God to redeem mankind. He didn't have to send His Son Jesus Christ to die for mankind. He sent Him, but at the same time Jesus did it voluntarily. If God was willing, it was the happy willingness of God.

According to the Scripture, we were made by God with tremendous intellectual and spiritual proportions. We have been made in the image of God. The thing that has destroyed this potential has been sin. It is this that brings us to a sense of orphanage.

As a consequence of this, the devil takes advantage of us and whispers his lie into the ear of man: "You do not really matter to God. God does not have any emotional connection with you. God isn't concerned about you."

And we believe that lie.

Contradicting this lie of Satan, the Christian message boasts, "God cares about you as an individual. No matter what the circumstances around your life at the present, God still cares about you."

I will make a little confession here. Whenever I get the feeling that

I'm important, and I speak and preach to a lot of important people, I do something to humble myself. Often, I will go into the inner city of Chicago to some of the old rescue missions and preach to the bums, the addicts and the homeless that gather there. As I look out over my ragtag congregation, I see individuals who have lost the sense of their individuality. They are caught up in the sociological statistics of their day.

There is a tramp in the second row. He is dressed in old ragged clothes that do not fit him too well. The shoes do not have laces in them and the one toe seems to be sticking out. He probably has not had a bath for a long time and reeks of dirt and cooties. There he is, smelling of every place he has been the last 10 years.

If I could catch him at a sober moment, I think he might say, "Why am I here? Nobody cares; I don't mean anything to anybody. There isn't anybody, anywhere, who has any emotional concern about me."

And to be truthful about it, his father's gone, his mother's gone, his family will not have anything more to do with him for various reasons. Everybody tries to forget that he is even alive. When the police officers find him lying in the alley, they say, "Move on, buddy."

There he sits, in a deep sense of sadness and orphanage with nothing to live for and nobody to care if he dies. He means nothing to anybody; nobody is concerned about his welfare; nobody cares what happens to him.

But that is not the end of the story. It does not have to stop here. The Christian evangel says, "For God so loved the world."

It says, you—dirt and whiskers and smell and filth—you wait a minute. Somebody is emotionally concerned about you. Somebody is not happy because you are the way you are. Somebody even knows your name, remembers you and loves you. You mean something to somebody.

Although our tramp may shake his foggy head in disbelief, the Christian message can get to him. "God so loved you that He gave His only begotten Son that whoever would—and you are included—believe in Him should not perish but have everlasting life. I am here from God to tell you that you do matter. Somebody cares about you."

This is that high compression, that shining facet of the diamond of truth, which God has thrown out to the world almost with happy carelessness and said, "Take it."

A mother doesn't have to get up and feed her baby at two in the morning. There's no law compelling her to do it. The law probably would compel her to take some care of the little tyke, but she doesn't have to give him that loving care that she does. She wants to do it. I used to do it for our little fellows, and I enjoyed doing it. A mother and a father do what they do because they love to do it.

The incarnation, too, was not something that Jesus Christ did gritting His teeth and saying, "I hate this thing—I wish I could get out of it." One of the dear old hymn writers said, "He abhorred not the virgin's womb." The writer thought about this and said, "Wait a minute here. The womb of the creature? How could the everlasting, eternal, infinite God, whom space cannot contain, confine Himself inside one of His creatures? Wouldn't it be a humiliation?"

Then he smiled and said, "No, He abhorred not the virgin's womb," and he wrote it and we've been singing it for centuries.

The incarnation of Jesus Christ's immortal flesh was not a heavy thing. The second person of the Trinity, the everlasting Son, the eternal Word, made Himself flesh—joyously! When the angels sang about the incarnation, they sang joyously about it.

And He also delights in salvation. Notice in Luke 15:5 that when Jesus Christ saves a man, He carries him on His shoulders. And what is the verb in that verse? It is *rejoicing!* God is not only pleased with Himself, delighted with His own perfection and happy in His work of creating and redeeming, but He is also enthusiastic. There is an enthusiasm in the Godhead, and there is enthusiasm in creation.

Grace And Mercy

Why were we not destroyed when we sinned? The only answer is that God of His goodness spared us. The cordial, kind-intentioned God spared us. Why would God the Eternal Son bleed for us? The answer is, out of His goodness and lovingkindness. *"Therefore the children of men put their trust under the shadow of thy wings."* (Psalm 36:7)

Why would God forgive me when I've sinned and then forgive me again and again? Because God out of His goodness acts according to that goodness and does what His loving heart dictates that He do.

Nobody ever got anything from God on the grounds that he deserved it. Having fallen, man deserves only punishment and death. So, if God answers prayer, it's because God is good. From His goodness, His lovingkindness, His good-natured benevolence, God does it! That's the source of everything.

These are the only grounds upon which anybody has ever been saved since the beginning of the world. There is an idea abroad that in the Old Testament men were saved by law and that in the New Testament we are saved by grace. The second is right, but the first is wrong. Nobody has ever been saved, from the day that Abel offered his bloody lamb on a homemade altar, down to the latest convert made today, except out of the goodness of God. Because of God's grace, His mercy, His lovingkindness, His goodness and graciousness, His cordiality and approachability, He kindly saved people. We've taken the word "grace" and made a technical term out of it.

The people in the Old Testament were not saved by keeping anything, because we deserved hell, and if God had acted according to justice alone, He simply would have pulled the stopper out and flushed us all down to hell and been done with it. But God out of His lovingkindness graciously forgave those who would come according to the conditions God laid down.

Everybody is saved by grace. Abel was saved by grace. Noah was saved by grace— *"Noah found grace in the eyes of the LORD"* (Genesis 6:8). So was Moses and all the rest down to the coming of Jesus and His dying on the cross. All were saved by grace out of the goodness of God.

And everybody's been saved by grace out of the goodness of God ever since.

Grace precedes everything—from the first day of creation until the Virgin Mary gave birth in a Bethlehem manger. For it was the grace of God in Christ that saved the human race from extinction when they sinned in the Garden. It was the grace of God in Jesus Christ yet to be born that saved the eighth person when the Flood covered the earth.

And it was the grace of God in Jesus Christ, yet to be born but existing in preincarnation glory, that forgave David when he committed his sin; that forgave Abraham when he lied; that enabled Abraham to pray God down to 10 righteous persons when He was threatening to destroy Sodom; that forgave Israel repeatedly.

It was the grace of God in Christ yet before the Incarnation that made God say, "*I have risen early in the morning and stretched out My hands unto you.*" It made him say, "*Like as a father pitieth his children, so the LORD pitieth them that fear him.*" (Ps. 103:13)

Jesus is the channel through which grace comes. And He said, "I am the truth," and it is through Him that grace is released to the world, through His wounded side, to sinners like you and me. All the grace of God anywhere comes through Jesus Christ. Then he says, "*No man hath seen God at any time; the only begotten Son, which is in the bosom of the Father, he hath declared him.*" (John 1:18)

The mercy of God is infinite too, and the man who has felt the grinding pain of inward guilt knows that this is more than academic. "*Where sin abounded, grace did much more abound.*" Abounding sin is the terror of the world, but abounding grace is the hope of mankind. However sin may abound it still has its limits, for it is the product of finite minds and hearts; but God's "much more" introduces us to infinitude. Against our deep creature-sickness stands God's infinite ability to cure.

The Christian witness through the centuries has been that "God so loved the world…". It remains for us to see that love in the light of God's infinitude. His love is measureless. It is more; it is boundless. It has no bounds because it is not a thing but a facet of the essential nature of God. His love is something He is, and because He is infinite that love can enfold the whole created world in itself and have room for ten thousand times ten thousand worlds beside.

This, this is the God we adore,

Our faithful, unchangeable Friend,

Whose love is as great as His power,

And neither knows measure nor end.

'Tis Jesus, the first and the last,

Whose Spirit shall guide us safe home;

We' praise Him for all that is past,

And trust Him for all that's to come.

Joseph Hart

The familiar picture of God as often torn between His justice and His mercy is altogether false to the facts. To think of God as inclining first toward one and then toward another of His attributes is to imagine a God who is unsure of Himself, frustrated and emotionally unstable, which of course is to say that the one of whom we are thinking is not the true God at all but a weak, mental reflection of Him badly out of focus.

All of God's acts are consistent with all of His attributes. No attribute contradicts the other, but all harmonize and blend into each other in the infinite abyss of the Godhead. All that God does agrees with all that God is, and being and doing are one in Him.

Full, Fair and Many Means

Let me quote from the book by Lady Julian: "God of His goodness has ordained means to help us, full, fair and many; the chief being that which He took upon Him, the nature of man." In coming to earth as a man, God came where we were, and by coming where we were He understands us by sympathy and empathy.

Sympathy is a good old-fashioned country word: *-pathy* has the same root as *pathos*, which means "feeling or suffering often"; *sym-* means "together," such as in the word *symphony* (a group of musicians playing *together* in harmony). Sympathy, then, is God feeling and suffering along with us. Empathy, of course, is a bit different. It means the ability to project yourself into somebody else and feel as he feels. It is a wonderful theme, and every old grandmother on any old farm in Tennessee knows what empathy means. But it took a good scientist to give it a name.

Let me read it for you from the Bible—in biblical language instead of in the language of psychology:

Wherefore in all things it behoved him [that is, when He took on Him the seed of Abraham] to be made like unto his brethren, that he might be a merciful and faithful high priest in things pertaining to God, to make reconciliation for the sins of the people. For in that he himself hath suffered being tempted, he is able to succour them that are tempted. (Hebrews 2:17-18)

We have not an high priest which cannot be touched with the feeling of our infirmities; but was in all points tempted like as we are, yet without sin. Let us therefore come boldly unto the throne of grace, that we may obtain mercy, and find grace to help in time of need. (4:15-16)

These are passages full of empathy. Not only does He feel along with us in our wretchedness, but He is also able to project Himself into us, so He knows how we feel and can feel with us. That is good theology.

Now God of His goodness has ordained means, "full, fair and many." And it was all out of God's goodness. We say sometimes, "The justice of God requires Him to do so and so." Never use that language—even if you hear me using it! There is never anything that *requires* God to do anything. God does what He does because of what He is, and there is not something standing outside of Him requiring Him to do something. He does what He does out of His own heart. All the attributes of God are simply facets of one God in three Persons.

What are these "full, fair and many" means God has made for His people? They are the precious amends that He's made for man's sins, "turning all our blame into endless worship."

Sometimes I say things to God in prayer which are terribly bold, almost arrogant, and I've never been rebuked by God yet. They said about Luther (I'm certainly not drawing any comparison; I'd have been glad to clean his shoes and put them at his bedroom door!) that when they heard him pray it was an experience in theology. When he began to pray, he prayed with such self-abnegation, such humility, such repentance that you pitied him. But as he prayed on, he prayed with such boldness that you feared for him.

Sometimes in my private prayers I've gone to God with thoughts that I hesitate to mention, but I'm going to mention this one. Only last Friday I said to God in prayer: "I'm glad I sinned, God; I'm glad I sinned, for Thou didst come to save sinners." (see 1 Timothy 1:15)

I'm not a good man; I'm a—well, you'd have to use slang to describe me! By nature I come that way. And when I saw it in my boys, I didn't blame them. I paddled them, but I didn't blame them. I can't go to God and say, "God, I didn't do what that fellow did." I've done everything—either in actuality or in thought—that could be done. The devil himself couldn't have thought of anything that I haven't thought of in my lifetime.

So I was praying to God about it and I said, "O God, these good men"—and I began naming men who, compared with me, are good men— "they can't love You as much as I do, for he who is forgiven much loves much." (see Luke 7:47)

If a doctor saves a man who has only a runny nose, he wouldn't write a book about it. He didn't do much. The fellow would get well anyhow. But the doctor who takes a man with a brain tumor, puts him asleep and, with great care, prayer and skill, brings that man back to life—he has done something.

He "saved a wretch like me." He "turned all our blame into endless worship." I believe the Bible teaches—our Lord hinted at it and Paul developed it further—that the day will come when they will gather around us from everywhere, and say, "Behold the marvels of God." You read in the book of Acts (Acts 4:14) of seeing the man that was healed standing among them, and they could say nothing. And seeing that wicked sinner standing there, we can only say, "Worthy is the Lamb that was slain" (Revelation 5:12). And worthy is the goodness of God that out of His infinite kindness, His unchanging, perfect lovingkindness, He made amends for us, "full, fair and many," turning all our sin into endless worship.

4. The Faith of the Disciple

Restored Faith for Restored Communion

"Without faith it is impossible to please God" has become an axiom of the Christian way. Yet I suppose not many stop to ask why faith should be so vitally important in our relation with God. But there is a reason.

This is a moral universe. At bottom it is not material, though it contains matter; it is not mathematical, though it involves numbers. The God who made the world is a moral being and He has filled His world with moral creatures.

We hear of mysterious beings who have access to the presence of God and who range throughout the whole creation as servants of the Most High. "Bless the Lord, ye his angels, that excel in strength, that do his commandments, hearkening unto the voice of his word." The Scriptures tell us of at least four orders of such beings and refer to what they call "watchers and holy ones," which may indicate other orders or may simply refer to the previously mentioned four.

In addition, there is another and of course a more familiar order of being, the last and (before his fall) the highest of all the creatures God created and made. I refer to man who was made in God's image and likeness and who for that reason bears toward God a unique moral and spiritual relation.

Because this is a moral universe, character, which is the excellence of moral beings, is naturally paramount. As the excellence of steel is strength, and the excellence of art is beauty, so the excellence of mankind is moral character.

"An honest man is the noblest work of God," an apothegm usually attributed to John Wesley, may sound at first rather extreme, but if we allow the word "honest" to stand for all the moral virtues we may be able to understand the apothegm and possibly to agree with it. A saint should be not only a man of intense spiritual devotion but a man of symmetrical virtues and perfectly balanced character.

Relationship between moral beings is by confidence, and confidence rests upon character, which is a guarantee of conduct. It is true that sin has introduced confusion into the world so that we do not always find consistency of moral conduct among men. Yet, to live in a moral world, it is necessary that we put confidence in our fellow man. A complete breakdown of confidence would destroy the adhesive quality of society, tear apart the fabric of civilization and turn the world into a cage of savage beasts. However bad men may become at times, they must still trust each other. It is either confidence or chaos.

What has all this to do with faith in God? Just this: God is a being of supreme moral excellence, possessing in infinite perfection all the qualities that constitute holy character. He deserves and invites the unreserved confidence of every moral creature, including man. Any proper relation to Him must be by confidence, that is, by faith. Where there is no faith, it is impossible to please God.

Human sin began with loss of faith in God. When our mother Eve listened to Satan's sly innuendoes against the character of God, she began to entertain a doubt of His integrity, and right there the doors were opened to the incoming of every possible evil, and darkness settled upon the world.

The Bible talks about man's being alienated from and an enemy to God. Should this sound harsh or extreme, you have only to imagine your closest personal friend coming to you and stating in cold seriousness that he no longer has any confidence in you. "I do not trust you. I have lost confidence in your character. I am forced to suspect every move you make."

Such a declaration would instantly alienate friends by destroying the foundation upon which every friendship is built. Until your former friend's opinion of you had been reversed there could be no further communion. Only a restored faith could bring about a restored friendship.

Now, it is well known that people do not go boldly to God and profess that they have no confidence in Him, and no one except the rare professional unbeliever is willing to witness publicly to his low view of God. The frightful thing, however, is that people everywhere act out their unbelief with a consistency that is more convincing than words.

Idolatry is the supreme sin and unbelief is the child of idolatry. Both are libels on the character of the Most High and the Most Holy. "He that believeth not God hath made him a liar," wrote the apostle John.

A God who lies is a God without character, and where there is no character there can be no confidence. This is the moral logic of unbelief. The unbeliever refuses to trust God because his conception of God is base and ignoble. That he does not burn incense to a graven image does not make him less an idolater, unless we want to make a distinction and say that the idolater worships his false god while the unbeliever refuses to do even that.

The joyous message of Christianity is that there is a way back from this place of unbelief and alienation. "He that cometh to God must believe that he is, and that he is a rewarder of them that diligently seek him." The gospel message declares that the wronged God took the wrong upon Himself in order that the one who committed the wrong might be saved.

Repentance is, among other things, a sincere apology to God for distrusting Him so long, and faith is throwing oneself upon Christ in complete confidence. Thus, reconciliation is achieved between God and man by faith.

Belief Through Christ

In 1 Peter 1:21 it says, "*Who by him do believe in God.*" There can be no true believing in God apart from Christ. Out in the world, a great many people believe in God. You can see it in the newspapers, the Saturday magazines and in many of our bestseller books. A number of religious books have become bestsellers and are sold in drugstores. The publishers are saying a wonderful new something is taking place. People are interested in religion. One magazine had an essay that the world could be saved by religion and gave the various religions, and Christianity was one of them.

If the Bible is God's book, and Peter was God's apostle, and this New Testament is divinely inspired, then I am led to conclude that real belief in God can come only through Christ. Any other kind of faith in God or belief about God is spotty, imperfect, perverted and very often erroneous.

Some things we can know about God with certainty. We can know His eternal power and Godhead. The American Indian standing on the shore of the lake raises his arms to the Great Spirit, evoking the help of the Great Spirit on his hunting trip. That was an approach to

God of some sort and was some kind of belief. Thomas Edison is reputed to say that he believed God was force, and if he could live long enough, he believed he could invent an instrument sensitive enough to detect God. That was some kind of belief in God.

The deists, such as Voltaire and others, thought of God as a great principal, but He was not a great personality. That was some kind of belief in God. And the heathen in their blindness have some kind of belief in God. In the end, any belief in God is better than no belief in God. That is open to question, but at least for the moment, I give you my tentative statement that it is better to believe in God in a vague, shadowy way than not to believe there is a God.

Acquaintance with God

All things else being equal, the destiny of a man or nation may safely be predicted from the idea of God which that man or that nation holds. No nation can rise higher than its conception of God. While Rome held to her faith in the stern old gods of the Pantheon, she remained an iron kingdom. Her citizens unconsciously imitated the character of her gods, however erroneous their conception of the Deity might have been. When Rome began to think loosely about God she began to rot inwardly, and that rot never stopped till it brought her to the ground. So it must always be with men and nations.

A church is strong or weak just as it holds to a high or low idea of God. For faith rests not primarily upon promises, but upon character. A believer's faith can never rise higher than his conception of God. A promise is never better or worse than the character of the one who makes it. An inadequate conception of God must result in a weak faith, for faith depends upon the character of God, just as a building rests upon its foundation.

This explains why unbelief is such a grievous sin; it is pure libel against the Lord of heaven and earth. Unbelief judges God to be unworthy of confidence and withholds its trust from Him. Can there be a more heinous sin than this?

"He that believeth not God hath made him a liar." (1 John 5:10) Our hearts shrink from the full implications of such a statement, but would not this seem to teach that unbelief attributes to God the character of Satan? Jesus said of Satan, "He is a liar and the father of it."

Unbelief says virtually the same thing of God.

How then shall unbelief be cured and faith be strengthened? Surely not by straining to believe the Scriptures, as some do. Not by a frantic effort to believe the promises of God. Not by gritting our teeth and determining to exercise faith by an act of the will. All this has been tried—and it never helps. To try thus to superinduce faith is to violate the laws of the mind and to do violence to the simple psychology of the heart.

What is the answer? Job told us, "Acquaint thyself with him and be at peace"; and Paul said, "*So then faith cometh by hearing, and hearing by the word of God.*" These two verses show the way to a strong and lasting faith: Get acquainted with God through reading the Scriptures, and faith will come naturally. This presupposes that we come to the Scriptures humbly, repudiating self-confidence and opening our minds to the sweet operations of the Spirit.

Otherwise stated: Faith comes effortlessly to the heart as we elevate our conceptions of God by a prayerful digestion of His Word. And such faith endures, for it is grounded upon the Rock.

More on Faith

The second assertion is "*Let us hold fast our profession of faith*" (Heb. 10:23). We would like to get a spiritual experience floating us on high, above all. We would like to go into orbit and be sure there was nothing to do but simply ride around. You do not go to heaven that way.

I once noticed an ad for a pair of shoes. According to the ad, you put them on and just walk around on air. People imagine the Christian life the same way. You are converted, blessed and then walk around on air for the rest of your life. You do nothing of the sort.

I know there is a wheel in the middle of a wheel up there somewhere, but Christians do not happen to be in that place yet. So, we do not go to heaven on wheels, as the song says, "You Can't go to Heaven on Roller Skates." We cannot go to heaven any other way but by the simple, pedestrian way: walking by faith. The Lord does not talk about a flight of faith, nor does He talk about a tour of faith. He talks about a walk of faith.

The temptation to quit the journey comes to everybody. Some have been tempted to just give up the whole Christian life and be done with it. I suppose you feel very guilty about that, and you are; let me comfort you by telling you that you are not guilty all by yourself. People of God have that temptation come to them when things get tough, and they say, "What's the use of trying, anyhow? I can't do as I want to do, I can't serve God as I long to do." The temptation is to quit. But people are ashamed to admit it.

If their testimonies were as frank as they should be, many a man, instead of getting up and saying, "Pray for me that I may hold out faithful and so on," would say, "I was tempted last week to give up this whole deal, but the Lord helped me, and I didn't."

That would be frank; it would be a little difficult to do that, because we are taught to win friends and influence people and never tell the truth at all. We are trained to say the thing we are supposed to say rather than the honest thing. The pressure is just so great that we almost look up to God as Elijah did and say, "God, I've had it. There isn't any use, Father, take me; there's nobody around that's any good."

A Key to Holding Fast

We are tempted like that sometimes, but I have a little key for you. I usually do not hand out keys, but I have a little secret of how you hold fast the profession of your faith. It is so down-to-earth and common that it will disappoint you, but it is good. Just outlive your troubles. I have outlived so many things, so many people that did not like me; I just outlived them. You just go right on outliving your difficulties.

That neighbor who slams the door all hours of the night and morning and turns the TV on until it comes roaring through the partition until you say, "Oh, God, what will I do?" Just outlive him. He will move; you just keep right on where you are.

That neighbor whose dog howls incessantly, tied to a tree out there; just keep right on living. Go right on. He will move, God will take him somewhere else, and so with everything else that tempts you to want to quit.

How about that boss you work for that you just do not know how you can continue to go to work? You do not mind the work, but you just wish you were somewhere else, and you are shopping around for another job and cannot find one. You just keep right on walking with God, and one of these times something will happen. That fellow will be moved to some other town; he will get blessed; he will get to liking you or the problem will untangle. You just keep on; it will not kill you if you walk on with God.

"Let us hold fast," says the Word of God. But it also says, "to the profession of our faith." The profession of our faith has its ramifications right down in our living; so you just wait around, it will come out right.

A dear old brother with not too much education, but he was a dear saint, said the passage of Scripture he loved was, "It came to pass." He testified, "When I get in trouble, I just look up to God and say, 'Father, I remember this came to pass.'" It passes after a while, and all of your problems come to pass. They will pass if you'll just out-live them and keep right on.

5. The Meaning of Discipleship

I have been crucified with Christ and I no longer live, but Christ lives in me. The life I now live in the body, I live by faith in the Son of God, who loved me and gave himself for me.

GALATIANS 2:20

Highest Purpose in Redemption

There seems to be a great throng of professing Christians in our churches today whose total and amazing testimony sounds about like this: "I am thankful for God's plan in sending Christ to the cross to save me from hell." I am convinced that it is a cheap, low-grade, and misleading kind of Christianity that impels people to rise and state, "Because of sin, I was deeply in debt—and God sent His Son, who came and paid all my debts."

Of course, believing Christian men and women are saved from the judgment of hell, and it is a reality that Christ our Redeemer has paid the whole slate of debt and sin that was against us. But what does God say about His purposes in allowing Jesus to go to the cross and to the grave? What does God say about the meaning of death and resurrection for the Christian believer?

Surely, we know the Bible well enough to be able to answer that: God's highest purpose in the redemption of sinful humanity was based in His hope that we would allow Him to reproduce the likeness of Jesus Christ in our once-sinful lives! This is the reason why we should be concerned with this text—this testimony of the apostle Paul in which he shares his own personal theology with the Galatian Christians who had become known for their backslidings. It is a beautiful miniature, shining forth as an unusual and sparkling gem, an entire commentary on the deeper Christian life and experience. We are not trying to take it out of its context by dealing with it alone; we are simply acknowledging the fact that the context is too broad to be dealt with in any one message.

It is the King James Version of the Bible that quotes Paul: "I am crucified with Christ." Nearly every other version quotes Paul as speaking in a different tense: "I have been crucified with Christ," and that really is the meaning of it: "I have been crucified with Christ."

This verse is quoted sometimes by people who have simply memorized it and they would not be able to tell you what Paul was really trying to communicate. This is not a portion of Scripture that can be skipped through lightly. You cannot skim through and pass over this verse as many seem to be able to do with the Lord's Prayer and the twenty-third Psalm.

This is a verse with such depth of meaning and spiritual potential for the Christian believer that we are obligated to seek its full meaning— so it can become practical and workable and liveable in all of our lives in this present world.

It is plain in this text that Paul was forthright and frank in the matter of his own personal involvement in seeking and finding God's highest desires and provision for Christian experience and victory. He was not bashful about the implications of his own personality becoming involved with the claims of Jesus Christ. Not only does he plainly testify, "I have been crucified," but within the immediate vicinity of these verses, he uses the words I, myself, and me a total of fourteen times.

There certainly is, in the Bible, a good case for humility in the human personality, but it can be overdone. We have had a dear missionary veteran among us from time to time. He is learned and cultured—and overly modest. With a great wealth of missionary exploits and material to tell, he has always refused to use any first person reference to himself. When asked to tell about something that happened in his pioneer missionary life, he said: "One remembers when one was in China and one saw...."

That seems to be carrying the idea of modesty a bit too far, so I said to him, in a joking way, that if he had been writing the twenty-third Psalm, it would likely read: "The Lord is one's shepherd, one shall not want; He maketh one to lie down in green pastures. He leadeth one...."

I believe Paul knew that there is a legitimate time and place for the use of the word I. In spiritual matters, some people seem to want to maintain a kind of anonymity, if possible. As far as they are concerned, someone else should take the first step. This often comes up in the manner of our praying, as well. Some Christians are so general and vague and uninvolved in their requests that God Himself is unable to answer. I refer to the man who will bow his head and pray: "Lord, bless the missionaries and all for whom we should pray. Amen."

It is as though Paul says to us here, "I am not ashamed to use myself as an example. I have been crucified with Christ. I am willing to be pinpointed."

Only Christianity recognizes why the person who is without God and without any spiritual perception gets in such deep trouble with his own ego. When he says I, he is talking about the sum of his own individual being, and if he does not really know who he is or what he is doing here, he is besieged in his personality with all kinds of questions and problems and uncertainties.

Most of the shallow psychology religions of the day try to deal with the problem of the ego by jockeying it around from one position to another, but Christianity deals with the problem of I by disposing of it with finality.

The Bible teaches that every unregenerated human being will continue to wrestle with the problems of his own natural ego and selfishness. His human nature dates back to Adam. But the Bible also teaches with joy and blessing that every individual may be born again, thus becoming a "new man" in Christ.

When Paul speaks in this text, "I have been crucified," he is saying that "my natural self has been crucified." That is why he can go on to say, "Yet I live"—for he has become another and a new person— "I live in Christ and Christ lives in me."

It is this first I, the natural me, that stands confronted with the just anger of God. God cannot acknowledge and accept me as a natural and selfish man—I am unregenerate and an alien, the complete essence of everything that is anti-God!

I know there are men and women who dismiss the idea of anything being anti-God or anti-Christ. They are not willing to pay any heed to the teachings of Scripture relative to prophecy and eschatology.

Nevertheless, it is a biblical fact that whatever does not go through the process of crucifixion and transmutation, passing over into the new creation, is anti-Christ. Jesus said that all of that which is not with Christ is against Christ—those who are not on His side are against Him. We do not quite know what to do with those words of Christ, so we try to evade or work them over to a smooth, new version, but Jesus said *"he that gathereth not with me scattereth abroad"* (Matt. 12:30).

Tolerance Versus Charity

There is a great hue and cry throughout the world today on behalf of tolerance, and much of it comes from a rising spirit of godlessness in the nations. The communist nations, themselves the most intolerant, are preaching and calling for tolerance in order to break down all of the borders of religion and embarrass the American people with our social and racial problems.

This is the situation of the people of God: the most intolerant book in all the wide world is the Bible, the inspired Word of God, and the most intolerant teacher that ever addressed Himself to an audience was the Lord Jesus Christ Himself.

On the other hand, Jesus Christ demonstrated the vast difference between being charitable and being tolerant. Jesus Christ was so charitable that in His great heart He took in all the people in the world and was willing to die even for those who hated Him.

But even with that kind of love and charity crowning His being, Jesus was so intolerant that He taught: "If you are not on My side, you are against Me. If you do not believe that I am He, you shall die in your sins." He did not leave any middle ground to accommodate the neutral who preach tolerance. There is no "twilight zone" in the teachings of Jesus—no place in between.

Charity is one thing, but tolerance is quite another matter. Tolerance easily becomes a matter of cowardice if spiritual principles are involved, if the teachings of God's Word are ignored and forgotten.

Suppose we take the position of compromise that many want us to take: "Everyone come, and be saved if you want to. But if you do not want to be saved, maybe there is some other way that we can find for you. We want you to believe in the Lord Jesus Christ if you will, but if you do not want to, there may be a possibility that God will find some other way for you because there are those who say that there are many ways to God."

That would not be a spirit of tolerance on our part—it would be downright cowardice. We would be guilty with so many others of a spirit of compromise that so easily becomes an anti-God attitude.

True Christianity deals with the human problem of the self-life, with the basic matter of "me, myself, and I." The Spirit of God deals with it by an intolerant and final destruction, saying, "This selfish I cannot live if God is to be glorified in this human life." God Himself deals with this aspect of human nature—the sum of all our proud life—and pronounces a stern condemnation upon it, flatly and frankly disapproving of it, fully and completely rejecting it.

And what does God say about it? "I am God alone, and I will have nothing to do with man's selfish ego, in which I find the essence of rebellion and disobedience and unbelief. Man's nature in its pride of self and egotism is anti-God—and sinful, indeed!" It is in this matter of how to deal with man's proud and perverse and sinful human nature that we discover two positions within the framework of Christianity.

One position is that which leans heavily upon the practice of psychology and psychiatry. There are so-called Christian leaders who insist that Jesus came into the world to bring about an adjustment of our ego, our selfishness, our pride, our perversity. They declare that we may become completely adjusted to life and to one another by dealing with the complexes and the twisted concepts that we have gotten into because our mothers scolded us when we were babies! So there are thousands of referrals as the clergymen shift our problems from the church to the psychiatric couch.

On the other hand, thank God, the Bible plainly says that Jesus Christ came to bring an end of self—not to educate it or tolerate it or polish it! No one can ever say that Jesus Christ came to tell us how to cultivate our natural ego and pride. Jesus never taught that we could learn to get along with the big, proud I in our lives by giving it a love for Bach and Beethoven and Da Vinci.

Paul outlined the full spiritual remedy: "I am crucified with Christ ... and the life which I now live in the flesh I live by the faith of the Son of God, who loved me, and gave Himself for me." This is a decision and an attitude of faith and commitment called for in the life of every believing Christian.

Baptism: Death and Resurrection

When we see that Jesus Christ came into the world to deal effectively and finally with our life of self and egotism and pride, we must take a stand. With God's help, we say to that big I in our nature: "This is as far as you go—you are deposed. You are no longer to be in control!" In true repentance and in self-repudiation, we may turn our backs on the old self life. We may refuse to go along with it any longer. We have the right and the power to desert its ranks and cross over to spiritual victory and blessing on Emmanuel's side, walking joyfully under the banner of the cross of Jesus Christ from that hour on.

This is what it means to deal with and finally dispose of the "old man," the old life of self, which is still causing problems in so many Christian lives. We take a place of actual identification with Jesus Christ in His crucifixion, burial, and resurrection.

In the Christian life, that is what baptism is supposed to mean, but it is sad to say that baptism is nothing but a quick dip to the average person because that one does not know what baptism represents. He does not know that baptism genuinely ought to be an outward and visible testimony of a spiritual and inward transformation that has taken place; a symbol declaring that the old selfish and perverse human nature is repudiated in humility, and put away, crucified, declared dead!

That is what baptism should mean to the believer—death and burial with Christ, then raised with Him in the power of His resurrection! It can happen apart from water baptism of any mode, but that is what water baptism should indicate. It should set forth that identification with the death and resurrection of Jesus Christ just as a wedding ring witnesses and sets forth the fact that you are married.

Identification with Christ

Now, it is impossible to bring together and synchronize these two positions concerning the old life and nature of self. I do not believe that we are ever obliged to dovetail these two positions. Either the

Lord Jesus Christ came to bring an end of self and reveal a new life in spiritual victory, or He came to patch and repair the old self—He certainly did not come to do both!

I expect someone to say, "We are interested in spiritual victory and blessing in our group, but our approach doesn't agree with yours at all!"

In answer I can only say that on the basis of the Word of God, true identification with Jesus Christ in His death, burial and resurrection will lead men and women to Christlikeness. God has never promised to work out His image in us in a variety of ways according to the inclinations of our own group. Forming the likeness to Jesus Christ in human lives and personalities is something that He does alike in all groups and all conferences and all fellowships around the world regardless of what they may be called.

There really is no way to patch up and repair the old life of self. The whole burden of New Testament theology insists that the old human self is ruined completely. It has no basic goodness, it holds to false values and its wisdom is questionable, to say the least. It is the new self in Christ Jesus—the new man in Christ—that alone must live. Onward from the point of this commitment, we must reckon ourselves indeed to have died unto sin, to be alive unto God in Christ Jesus....

Human beings continue to lean on a variety of crutches to support the ego, to nourish the pride, to cover the obvious defects in human existence. Many have believed that continuing education would provide that missing link between personality and potential. Many have turned to the pursuits of philosophies; others to cultural achievements. Ancestry and environment and status occupy many more.

But the ability to brag about human ancestors, to point with pride to the nation of our descent or the cultural privileges we have known— these do not transform and change and regenerate the human nature. Regardless of our racial strains, regardless of our cultural and educational advantages, we are all alike as human beings. In my own nature, I am nothing. Of myself, I know nothing. In God's sight, without His help and His enabling, I have nothing and I can do nothing.

But the inventory of the new man in Christ Jesus is so different! If he has found the meaning of commitment, the giving up of self to be identified with Jesus Christ in His crucifixion and death, he discovers in an entirely new measure the very presence of Christ Himself!

This new person has made room for the presence of Christ, so there is a difference in the personal inventory. It is no longer the old do-nothing, know-nothing, be-nothing, have-nothing person! That old assertive self died when the crucified and risen Savior was given His rightful place of command and control in the personality. The old inventory cried out: "How can I be what I ought to be?" but the inventory of the new man is couched in faith and joy in his recognition that "Christ liveth in me!"

Paul expressed it to the Colossians in this way: "Christ in you, the hope of glory!" and then proceeded to assure them that "You are complete in Him!"

Paul wrote to the Ephesians to remind them that the essence of faith and hope in Christ is the assurance of being "accepted in the Beloved."

To the Corinthian believers, Paul promised full spiritual deliverance and stability in the knowledge that Jesus Christ "is made unto us wisdom, righteousness, sanctification and redemption."

Our great need, then, is simply Jesus Christ. He is what we need. He has what we need. He knows what we need to know. He has the ability to do in us what we cannot do—working in us that which is well-pleasing in God's sight.

This is a difficult point in spiritual doctrine and life for many people.

"What about my ambition? I have always been ambitious so it is a part of my being. Doesn't it matter?"

"I am used to doing my own thing in my own way—and I am still doing it in the church. Do I have to yield that?"

"I have always been able to put my best foot forward to get recognition and publicity. I am used to seeing my name in the paper. What do I get from crucifixion with Christ?"

Brothers and sisters, you get Christ and glory and fruitfulness and future and the world to come, whereof we speak, and the spirits of just men made perfect; you get Jesus, the Mediator of a new covenant, and the blood of the everlasting covenant; an innumerable company of angels and the church of the firstborn and the New Jerusalem, the city of the living God!

And before you get all that, you have the privilege and the prospect of loving and joyful service for Christ and for mankind on this earth.

This is a gracious plan and provision for men and women in the kindness and wisdom of God. He loves you too well and too much to let you continue to strut and boast and cultivate your egotism and feed your 'I'. He just cannot have that kind of selfish assertion in His children, so Jesus Christ works in us to complete Himself and make Himself anew in us.

So, you see, that is really why Jesus Christ came into this world to tabernacle with us, to die for us. God is never going to be done with us in shaping us and fashioning us as dear children of God until the day that we will see Him face to face, and His name shall be in our foreheads. In that day, we shall genuinely be like Him and we shall see Him as He is.

Truly, in that gracious day, our rejoicing will not be in the personal knowledge that He saved us from hell, but in the joyful knowledge that He was able to renew us, bringing the old self to an end, and creating within us the new man and the new self in which can be reproduced the beauty of the Son of God.

In the light of that provision, I think it is true that no Christian is where he ought to be spiritually until that beauty of the Lord Jesus Christ is being reproduced in daily Christian life. I admit that there is necessarily a question of degree in this kind of transformation of life and character.

Certainly there has never been a time in our human existence when we could look into our own being, and say: "Well, thank God, I see it is finished now. The Lord has signed the portrait. I see Jesus in myself!"

Nobody will say that—nobody!

Even though a person has become like Christ, he will not know it. He will be charitable and full of love and peace and grace and mercy and kindness and goodness and faithfulness—but he will not really know it because humility and meekness are also a part of the transformation of true godliness. Even though he is plainly God's man and Christ's witness, he will be pressing on, asking folks to pray for him, reading his Bible with tears, and saying, "Oh, God, I want to be like

Thy Son!"

God knows that dear child is coming into the likeness of His Son, and the angels know it, and the observing people around him know it, too. But he is so intent upon the will and desires of God for his life and personality that he does not know it, for true humility never looks in on itself. Emerson wrote that the eye that sees only itself is blind and that the eye is not to see with but to see through. If my eye should suddenly become conscious of itself, I would be a blind man.

Now, there is a practical application of the crucified life and its demands from day to day. John the Baptist realized it long ago when he said, "He must increase but I must decrease!"

There must necessarily be less and less of me—and more and more of Christ! That's where you feel the bite and the bitterness of the cross, brother! Judicially and potentially, I was crucified with Christ, and now God wants to make it actual. In actuality, it is not as simple as that. Your decision and commitment do not then allow you to come down from that cross. Peace and power and fruitfulness can only increase according to our willingness to confess moment by moment, "It is no longer I, but Christ that liveth in me."

God is constantly calling for decisions among those in whom there is such great potential for displaying the life of Jesus Christ. We must decide: "My way, or Christ's?" Will I insist upon my own righteousness even while God is saying that it must be the righteousness of His Son? Can I still live for my own honor and praise? No, it must be for Christ's honor and praise to be well-pleasing to God. "Do I have any choice? Can I have my own plan?" No, God can only be honored as we make our choices in Christ and live for the outworking of God's plan.

Modern theology refuses to press down very hard at this point, but we still are confronted often with spiritual choices in our hymnology. We often sing: "Oh, to be dead to myself, dear Lord; Oh, to be lost in Thee."

We sing the words, we soon shut the book, and drift away with friends to relax and have a pleasant soda. The principle does not become operative in most Christians. It does not become practical. That is why I keep saying and teaching and hoping that this principle that is objective truth will become subjective experience in Christian lives. For any professing Christian who dares to say, "Knowing the truth

is enough for me; I do not want to mix it up with my day-to-day life
and experience," Christianity has become nothing but a farce and a
delusion!

It may surprise you that Aldous Huxley, often a critic of orthodox and
evangelical Christianity, has been quoted as saying: "My kingdom go
is the necessary correlary to Thy kingdom come."

How many Christians are there who pray every Sunday in church,
"Thy kingdom come! Thy will be done!" without ever realizing the
spiritual implications of such intercession? What are we praying for?
Should we edit that prayer so that it becomes a confrontation: "My
kingdom go, Lord; let Thy kingdom come!" Certainly His kingdom
can never be realized in my life until my own selfish kingdom is deposed. It is when I resign, when I am no longer king of my domain
that Jesus Christ will become king of my life.

Now, brethren, in confession, may I assure you that a Christian clergyman cannot follow any other route to spiritual victory and daily
blessing than that which is prescribed so plainly in the Word of God.
It is one thing for a minister to choose a powerful text, expound it and
preach from it—it is quite something else for the minister to honestly
and genuinely live forth the meaning of the Word from day to day. A
clergyman is a man—and often he has a proud little kingdom of his
own, a kingdom of position and often of pride and sometimes with
power. Clergymen must wrestle with the spiritual implications of the
crucified life just like everyone else, and to be thoroughgoing men of
God and spiritual examples to the flock of God, they must die daily to
the allurements of their own little kingdoms of position and prestige.

One of the greatest of the pre-Reformation preachers in Germany
was Johannes Tollar, certainly an evangelical before Luther's time.
The story has been told that a devout layman, a farmer whose name
was Nicholas, came down from the countryside, and implored Dr.
Tollar to preach a sermon in the great church, dealing with the deeper
Christian life based on spiritual union with Jesus Christ.

The following Sunday Dr. Tollar preached that sermon. It had 26
points, telling the people how to put away their sins and their selfishness in order to glorify Jesus Christ in their daily lives. It was a good
sermon—actually, I have read it and I can underscore every line of it.

When the service was over and the crowd had dispersed, Nicholas
came slowly down the aisle.

He said, "Pastor Tollar, that was a great sermon and I want to thank you for the truth which you presented. But I am troubled and I would like to make a comment, with your permission."

"Of course, and I would like to have your comment," the preacher said.

"Pastor, that was great spiritual truth that you brought to the people today, but I discern that you were preaching it to others as truth without having experienced the implications of deep spiritual principles in your own daily life," Nicholas told him. "You are not living in full identification with the death and resurrection of Jesus Christ. I could tell by the way you preached—I could tell!"

The learned and scholarly Dr. Tollar did not reply. But he was soon on his knees, seeking God in repentance and humiliation. For many weeks he did not take the pulpit to preach—earnestly seeking day after day the illumination of the Spirit of God in order that objective truth might become a deep and renewing and warming spiritual experience within.

After the long period of the dark sufferings in his soul, the day came when John Tollar's own kingdom was brought to an end and was replaced by God's kingdom. The great flood of the Spirit came in on his life and he returned to his parish and to his pulpit to become one of the greatest and most fervent and effective preachers of his generation. God's gracious blessings came—but Tollar first had to die. This is what Paul meant when he said, "I have been crucified with Christ."

This must become living reality for all of us who say we are interested in God's will for our lives. You pray for me and I will surely pray for you—because this is a matter in which we must follow our Lord!

We can quote this text from memory, but that is not enough. I can say that I know what Paul meant, but that is not enough. God promises to make it living reality in our lives the instant that we let our little, selfish kingdom go!

6. The Joy of the Disciple

Whom having not seen, ye love; in whom, though now ye see him not, yet believing, ye rejoice with joy unspeakable and full of glory.

1 PETER 1:8

Belief in the Invisible

Of all the apostles, Simon Peter, in my opinion, looms ahead of them all. His life and ministry are quite interesting to pursue. One of the most colorful of the disciples, he was the most vocally devoted to his Lord and ready to die for Him.

I could raise some concern about some of his attitudes and actions revealed to us in Scripture, but down deep inside, Peter was radically committed to the Lord Jesus Christ, which is why I hold him in such admiration. He did not often know how to show his love, but after that mighty day of Pentecost (see Acts 2), Peter, along with the rest of the disciples, was never the same again. He became a mighty force for God.

His writings are not eloquent like those of the apostle Paul's, for he takes a rather down-to-earth approach to Christianity. His words do not rise up in moments of ecstasy and oratory as Paul's often did, but they have a way of presenting truth that the average Christian can grasp. By reading his epistles, I can almost hear him preaching simple and practical Bible sermons. In the language of the common man, Peter tells in his epistles about this amazing, indestructible Christian, of which he is a part, who believes even when he cannot see that in which he believes.

In 1 Peter 1:8, Peter begins his description of this amazing Christian. He uses two expressions very much alike except in tense: "whom having not seen" and "now ye see him not." "Having not seen" has to do with any possibility of seeing Him in the past, and "now ye see him not" has to do with any possibility of seeing Him now.

Christians are God's by sanctification of the Spirit and having been sprinkled with the blood of Christ. They are believers in that which they cannot see and that which they have not seen. An old proverb says, "Seeing is believing."

Of course, there is a kind of believing that must depend upon seeing. However, it is merely a conclusion drawn from the testimony of the senses. This is not New Testament believing at all. New Testament believing believes a report about things unseen, which is the difference between New Testament faith and every other kind of so-called believing.

These Christians believed in the invisible, another way of stating it, and this brings it close to Hebrews 11:27: "*By faith he forsook Egypt, not fearing the wrath of the king: for he endured, as seeing him who is invisible.*" Abraham was able to endure because he was looking at the things that were invisible.

Being what we are, we pretty much trust what we can physically see; but if we could see all around us, if we could see the wonders, the invisible things of the creation, we would never be lonely for a moment and we would never doubt what is unseen. The invisible things are there, but they are simply not seen without faith. Abraham had faith and was able to carry on because he could see that which was not seen and could not be seen. And in so doing, these Christians mentioned in 1 Peter experienced the invisible so vividly and so satisfyingly that they were able to rejoice with joy unspeakable and full of glory.

Today we sing songs that are so dishonest that I sometimes hesitate to sing them. Yet when we sing the average hymn, if God Almighty compelled us to be entirely 100 percent honest, we simply could not sing them because their words would not be true of us.

Let me offer the words of a few hymns as examples. Here are the words of one song we sing often in our churches: "My faith looks up to Thee, Thou Lamb of Calvary, Savior divine!" It is a beautiful song written by Ray Palmer (1808–1887). When he wrote the last line— "O bear me safe above, a ransomed soul!" Palmer said, "I was so moved by what I was writing and what I was thinking about, that the last verse was written in a flood of tears."

That man meant it, but I wonder how many of us mean it when we sing that hymn today? It is only by a charitable adaptation of the truth that we are able to sing most of the hymns we sing.

"Love Divine, All Loves Excelling," written by Charles Wesley (1707-1788), is another hymn we sing with very little meaning.

Love divine, all loves excelling,

Joy of heaven to earth come down;

Fix in us thy humble dwelling;

All thy faithful mercies crown!

Jesus, Thou art all compassion,

Pure unbounded love Thou art;

Visit us with Thy salvation;

Enter every trembling heart.

I remember an old camp meeting song popular years ago, "Like a Mighty Sea," written by A. I. Zelley:

Like a mighty sea, like a mighty sea,

Comes the love of Jesus sweeping over me;

The waves of glory roll, the shouts I can't control;

Comes the love of Jesus sweeping o'er my soul.

I can easily believe that the brother who wrote those words was so lost in the grace of God that when he said, "The waves of glory roll, the shouts I can't control," he was literally telling the truth. Yet, many who sing "the shouts I can't control" can control their shouts easier than they can control their lust and their temper.

If the average Christian were to sing, "The waves of glory roll, my tongue I can't control," he would be telling the truth. But to say, "The shouts I can't control" is to lie in the face of God Almighty.

Yet we do an awful lot of lying. I suggest if you cannot feel it, do not sing it. Let us compromise and put it like this: let us sing it saying in our hearts, "Oh, God, it isn't true, but I want it to be true. It isn't so, Lord, but please make it so." I think God would understand and honor our desire.

If he or she is honest, the average Christian will sing, "See how I grovel here below, fond of these earthly toys," rather than sing, "The waves of glory roll, my shouts I can't control." How can we become the ones who sing in honesty "My shouts I can't control"?

The Christians that Peter writes about saw the invisible, believed in it and rejoiced with "joy unspeakable and full of glory." I do not know how to tell you how to get it; I only know how they got it. They got it by believing in what they could not see, and that is the only way that you and I will ever have joy unspeakable and a shout that we cannot control.

The characteristic of a Christian that Peter is trying to establish here is that he believes in things he cannot see. This Christian believes in the invisible. He believes that the real world coexists with the physical world, touching this world and accessible to this world. There is never any contradiction between spirit and reality. The contradiction is between spirit and matter, never between the spiritual and the real.

So the believer accepts and believes in a real world of which God is the King—an eternal kingdom, an eternal world, a spiritual and invisible world coexisting with and touching and accessible to this world. Heaven is not so far away that we must take a jet and continue through light years of travel to get to heaven. The average Christian thinks of heaven as being so far away, and only by accommodation do we sing about heaven being near and "glory coming down our souls to greet."

The Coexistent Worlds

The eternal world of which God is the King is inhabited by immortal spirits and has taken our dead Christian loved ones for a little time out of our sight. That world is as real—more real, in fact—than the physical world with which we are so very familiar.

There is a wonderful sense of coexisting in our world. This is not like the great vacuum gap between the stars in the heavens. You see a star in the heavens, and between that star and the next star are a few million light years of space. The visible world that is all around us is not separated from those invisible things.

It is a commonly known fact that two things of equal density cannot occupy the same place at the same time. But here is something we must remember on the other side: Two things that are not of equal density may coexist in the same place at the same time.

For instance, if you are sitting in front of your fireplace with the fire blazing, there would be two things coexisting—light and heat. They are not equal density; they are not mutually exclusive; they are mutually compatible and are the two things coming out of that fireplace.

Consider also the sun in the heaven above. Two things come from the sun at the same time, coexisting with each other: heat and light. We are warmed by the sun and we are lighted by the sun. Light and heat do not exclude each other; they are compatible and entwined with each other and live together. Therefore, the world below that God has made, which we call nature, and the world above that God has made, which He calls heaven, are coexistent.

Not only are they coexistent with each other, but they also touch each other and are accessible to each other so that God could put a ladder upon the earth and have its top reach the sky with angels ascending and descending. The one world is accessible to the other world either way; the gates swing both directions so that God could send His only begotten Son down and He could carry Stephen up. We can send our prayers up, and the answers can come down. The two worlds touch and are coexistent and accessible one to the other.

This Christian that Peter writes about believes in the invisible world. And this distinguishes him from every kind of materialism. During holiday seasons, our media boasts of the spiritual. However, after the season is over, they go back to materialism. Even while they are celebrating the spiritual, they do it in a materialistic way.

The Christian, however, sharply distinguishes from all kinds of materialism. He does not put a lot of value in what he sees. He does not limit his belief to only what he is able to touch with his hands. He endures, seeing the invisible. The immaterialist is not ghostly and phantom, but spiritual. That which is spiritual has real existence but is spirit instead of matter. The Christian believes that and lives in the light of it, which distinguishes him forever from all brands of materialism.

It also distinguishes him from all kinds of superstition and idolatry. The idolater also believes in the invisible, but the difference is that a Christian is one whose faith in the invisible has been corrected and chastened and purified by divine revelation.

A heathen can kneel down before a stone and if he is an intelligent heathen, you might ask him, "Why do you worship that stone?" He could answer, "I don't; I worship the deity resident in the stone."

The Greeks used to kneel in front of Mount Olympus, and if you said to them, "Why are you worshiping Mount Olympus?" they would say, "We do not worship the mountain; we worship the gods in the mountain." Even today, there are those who will kneel before statues in churches, and if you ask them, "Why do you worship that image?" they say, "We don't worship that image, we worship God of whom that image reminds us."

It is entirely possible to be a believer in the invisible and not be a Christian. Many people fall into this category. But it is not possible to be a Christian and not believe in the invisible. It is possible to believe that there is some kind of spooky world somewhere that must be placated with rabbit's feet, strange sayings, chains around our neck and medallions and all sorts of things. That is a belief in the invisible, but it is a pagan, erroneous belief.

When Jesus Christ came and brought life and immortality to light through the Gospels, He stood up, opened His mouth and talked to us, correcting that false and sinful belief in superstitious things by telling us what the real world is. He was the only one who had ever been there to come back and tell us. Abraham died, and his body sleeps in the cave of the field of Machpelah, while his spirit is with God; but he has never been back to tell us what it is like. Jesus, however, has been there from eternity, and when He came to earth, He told us of things of heaven and chided us because we did not accept what He said.

So the Christian is not a materialist that only believes in the validity of all material things. He is not an idolater, believing only vaguely in the existence of another world. He believes in what he has been taught by the One who had been there and came across the threshold into our world, smelling of myrrh and aloes out of the ivory palaces (see Ps. 45:8), fragrant from the presence of the eternal King.

An Eternal Perspective

Not only does a Christian believe in the invisible world, but he also counts on it. He acts, plans and lives as one who counts on the reality of the invisible. On the opposite side, the man of the earth does not believe in another world, or if he believes in it, he nods dutifully toward the belief in another world, but he does not let it change his plans any. He acts just the same as if there were no other world. He lays his plans precisely the same as if there were no invisible world, and he continues to live as if heaven is a myth and does not exist.

But the Christian counts on the other world, so that the invisible presence of God in His eternal kingdom, and the spirits made perfect in the holy church of the first-born, and the Holy Ghost and the invisible world actually influence his life. The invisible actually shapes his plans, determines his habits, comforts, consoles and supports him.

It is a comforting thought that God is near us. It is a comforting thought that there are invisible worlds near us. It consoles us to know that when Jesus prayed in the garden of Gethsemane, angels came to comfort Him, and He could have had legions of angels by His side. Nothing has changed. As the poem "The Kingdom of God" by Francis Thompson (1859-1907) proclaims:

The angels keep their ancient places—

Turn but a stone and start a wing!

'Tis ye, 'tis your estranged faces,

That miss the many-splendored thing.

Our unbelieving hearts have missed "the many-splendored thing." Angels are still here. Our friends on the other side of the ecclesiastical stone hedge are great for angels and celebrate the angelic host almost any time, day or night. But I have a sneaking suspicion there is a closer relation between their concept of angels and the pagan concept of Mount Olympus than there is of the New Testament concept. Because they go in big for Saint Angels, we do not need to turn our backs on angels and say they are not here. They are here, and Jesus said about the little child, *"Take heed that ye despise not one of these little ones; for I say unto you, that in heaven their angels do always behold the face of my Father which is in heaven.*" (Matt. 18:10)

Because pagan religion has mixed with Christianity and has created a perverted and false view of the angelic ministry, that is no reason for turning our backs on the whole thing. That the Muslims pray falsely and dutifully five times a day is no reason for me not to pray. That the Mormons have their Book of Mormon is no reason I am going to kick the Bible out into the alley. That the Christian Scientists meet in a church building is no reason why I am going tear some church building down. The fact of counterfeit should never force us to throw out the real thing.

Look at a real quarter and you read the words "Liberty, In God We Trust." On the other side is "United States of America, E Pluribus Unum, Quarter Dollar." I have never to my knowledge handled a counterfeit quarter, but if I had a counterfeit quarter and somebody pitched it back to me and said it was counterfeit, I would not take out all my quarters and throw them out in the back yard. Just because there is counterfeit abroad is no reason why I should reject the truth. If some people make too much of angels, that is no reason why I should get even with them and speak too little of them.

Quaker educator Thomas Kelly pointed out that we live on two planes: the plane of the natural and the plane of the spiritual. That is why a Christian is such a wonderful, weird, strange and puzzling creature. He is both animal and spirit, insisting upon living for the spiritual while down here in his mortal body, making a Christian a funny fellow.

Take for example, two men living on the same street together at number 1631 and number 1633, side by side. They are as different as night and day. One is a good-natured, easygoing, relaxed, downright old sinner on his way to hell but does not believe it. He is easy to get along with, bothers nobody, is friendly and waves when he goes down the street. He is a sinner, an Esau, a good-natured rebel on his way to hell.

Living alongside of him is a Christian, one that has been born again and has been given the blessed Holy Ghost as the wedding ring, but he has his troubles. He weeps when there is nothing to weep about and is moody when there is no reason. He is preoccupied when somebody is standing next to him wanting to talk. When the man next door cannot keep his radio off, he's worried about whether there has been bombing overseas. He may put his Bible under his arm and start off somewhere to a street meeting or to a prayer meeting. He is not as comfortable a fellow as the sinner is, and he does not act quite the same.

Why? Because the sinner lives on only one plane—the physical—and the Christian lives on two planes—the physical and the spiritual. In his body, he is down here in the flesh; but in his spirit, he is up yonder with God. And the result is that he is not as comfortable to be around as he might be. I have always said prophets are never comfortable people to have around, but they are indispensable if we are not going to rot.

It is characteristic of the Christian to be preoccupied with the invisible. Let me use the Lord's Supper as an illustration.

What is a sacrament? A sacrament is where the invisible meets and touches the visible. Eternal meets and touches the temporal. The Lord's Supper is a sacrament wherein we use the material as a thin garment to disguise the spiritual, and we use the temporal as a plate upon which we serve the eternal. That has always been the belief of the Christian.

There are two schools of thought that center on the sacrament of the Lord's Supper. The first is that the elements actually become visible—the invisible becomes visible—and that when you take the bread from the tray, you are touching consciously and lifting the very body that Mary gave to Jesus. That seems unworthy of a serious answer.

The second school of thought believes the invisible is present in, underneath and behind the visible, and I believe in that. Wherever faith has eyes to see, there is a smiling presence of the Son of God.

I believe that in the Lord's Supper, in the bread and the wine, we can trace it, we can know where it came from; we bought it. There is nothing magical about it. It could be fed to the birds; any sinner could drink the cup; there is nothing magical about it, but it is an object lesson. It sets forth in material terms the spiritual. It sets forth in temporal terms the eternal. And wherever faith is present, we touch and handle things unseen.

An illustration of this would be in the celebration of the Lord's Table. Even in the Early Church, some Christians became so engrossed with material things that they failed to recognize the spiritual. They drank the wine and enjoyed it and ate the bread and were full, but in so doing they did not have faith in the invisible. They were not discerning the Lord's body. (see 1 Cor. 11:29-30)

Throughout the Scripture, especially in the writings of the apostle Paul, the believers were warned about eating and drinking the Lord's Supper as a mere carnal thing. For many it became just a meal set before them to enjoy. This materialistic thinking grieved God. The Lord's Supper is more than just material elements; rather, for the man or woman of faith it is through this material gateway that we reach the spiritual.

The spiritual and the invisible and the eternal are right here. Faith recognizes that. This amazing Christian that Peter writes about puts his faith in the invisible, in that which he has not seen, so that the invisible has become visible. An old saint of God whom I once knew lived a rather simple life and refused to say things that were not true. Unlike him, many Christians boast that they never have a doubt. The hypocrites. They do have doubts, but they will not admit it.

This old man of God once testified, "I admit that I have doubts sometimes. I'll hear an argument or somebody will bounce an idea, and it'll stun me for a little. When I have such doubts I always dive down to the bottom and examine the foundation of my faith, and every time I've done it I've always come to the surface singing, 'How firm a foundation, ye saints of the Lord, is laid for your faith in his excellent Word.' "

> *How firm a foundation, ye saints of the Lord,*
>
> *Is laid for your faith in His excellent Word!*
>
> *What more can He say than to you He hath said,*
>
> *You, who unto Jesus for refuge have fled?*
>
> —John Rippon (1751-1836)

The Christian knows that he is saved, even though many things about his salvation are beyond his comprehension, but not beyond his trust. The truth he hangs on to has withstood centuries of attack without wavering. Standing upon this foundation, the Christian never wavers about his salvation but bows his head in humble appreciation of the amazing grace of God.

7.The Obedience of the Disciple

If we are alert enough to hear God's voice, we must not content ourselves with merely "believing" it. How can any man believe a command? Commands are to be obeyed, and until we have obeyed them, we have done exactly nothing at all about them. And to have heard them and not obeyed them is infinitely worse than never to have heard them at all, especially in the light of Christ's soon return and the judgment to come.

Dedicated

It is one of the ironies of modern life that after a word has been dropped from the Christian vocabulary because it no longer express-es any vital content in current church religion, it is often taken up by the world and made to mean not the same thing but something close to what it once meant in its original Christian usage.

Such a word is *dedicate*. This word in its various forms was once used to express a sacred idea deriving straight from the Scriptures. Though the exact English word is not found in our Authorized Version, the idea runs from Genesis to Revelation and all through Jewish and Christian history.

A noticeable change has come over the word in recent years, a semantic degeneration that has secularized it almost completely, and oddly enough the dictionary definitions unwittingly follow the word down: "Dedicate. 1. To devote to the service or worship of a divine being. 2. To set apart to a definite use or service. 3. To inscribe by way of compliment as a book." That is the way a late dictionary puts it, and in so doing furnishes its own spiritual commentary.

Now I have no quarrel with mere words. Whatever current usage and an up-to-date dictionary declare a word to mean, that is what it means, whatever it may have meant before. But I am concerned when men mistake earth for heaven, confuse this world with the world to come, and borrow sacred words to describe secular things—all without knowing what they have done. That is precisely what has happened to the word *dedication*. Through a radical change of meaning, it has been lost to the language of worship.

And it is highly significant that, up to this moment, Christians have not felt sufficient inward pressure to create a new word that would mean what the old word once meant. Apparently not only the word is gone from us, but the idea as well.

One reason for this is the current imperfect understanding of the Christian message. Scarcely anyone catches the imperious note in Christ's words. The Christian message has ceased to be a pronounce-ment and has become a proposition. Its invitational element has been pressed far out of proportion in the total scriptural scheme. Christ with His lantern, His apologetic stance and His weak pleading face has taken the place of the true Son of Man whom John saw clothed with a garment down to the foot, girt with a golden girdle, whose head and hair are white like wool, whose eyes are as a flame of fire, whose feet are like burnished brass and whose voice is as the sound of many waters.

The Christ of the tentative smile and air of puzzlement is not the Christ of God. The artists have been guilty of inadvertent idolatry in presenting to the world a false image of Christ. Only the Holy Spirit can reveal our Lord as He really is, and He does not paint in oils. He manifests Christ to the human spirit, not to our physical eyes.

Any public figure who is honest and who takes his job seriously is sure to be called a "dedicated man" by some reporter or news com-mentator. The word is even used to describe persons deeply con-cerned about wildlife refuges or the conservation of natural resourc-es. It is also applied to ball players and stock car racers, and not long ago a young bullfighter enthusiast spoke to me in defense of that gory and perilous sport.

He explained simply that the Spanish matador risks his life in the bullring "because he is a dedicated man. The people want the thrill of seeing the bull killed and he puts his life in jeopardy to furnish that thrill for them." The "dedicated" matador would likely win some sort of prize for sheer absurdity and may be allowed to stand as the uncrowned champion of all those who seek to waste their lives in the most foolish way.

But dedication to vanity is not confined to bullfighters. The truth is, dedication of the life to anything or anyone short of God Himself is a prostitution of noble powers and must bring a harvest of grief and disappointment at last. Only God is worthy of the soul He has made in His own image. To devote our lives to any cause, however worthy, is to sell ourselves short. Not money, position, fame, can justly claim our devotion. Art, literature, music also fall short.

And, if God is forgotten, even the loftiest and most unselfish task is unworthy of the soul's full surrender. Complete dedication unto death in the cause of freedom, for instance, is a touching thing and has given to history many of her greatest heroes, but only the God of freedom should have our "last full measure of devotion."

These are strenuous times and men are being recruited everywhere to devote themselves to one or another master. Let us be careful. No one has any true right to claim my life except the One who gave His own life for my redemption. If He gets my full dedication then I may engage in any good and worthy cause under His Spirit's guidance. But anything short of complete devotion to Christ is inadequate and must end in futility and loss.

No Salvation without Obedience

The Scriptures do not teach that the person of Jesus Christ nor any of the important offices that God has given Him can be divided or ignored according to the whims of men. Therefore, I must be frank in my feeling that a notable heresy has come into being throughout our evangelical Christian circles—the widely accepted concept that we humans can choose to accept Christ only because we need Him as Savior and we have the right to postpone our obedience to Him as Lord as long as we want to!

This concept has sprung naturally from a misunderstanding of what the Bible actually says about Christian discipleship and obedience. It is now found in nearly all of our full gospel literature. I confess that I was among those who preached it before I began to pray earnestly, to study diligently and meditate with anguish over the whole matter.

I think the following is a fair statement of what I was taught in my early Christian experience and it certainly needs a lot of modifying and a great many qualifiers to save us from being in error. "We are saved by accepting Christ as our Savior; we are sanctified by accepting Christ as our Lord; we may do the first without doing the second!"

The truth is that salvation apart from obedience is unknown in the sacred Scriptures. Peter makes it plain that we are *"elect according to the foreknowledge of God the Father, through sanctification of the Spirit, unto obedience."* (1 Peter 1:2)

What a tragedy that in our day we often hear the gospel appeal made on this kind of basis: "Come to Jesus! You do not have to obey anyone. You do not have to change anything. You do not have to give up anything, alter anything, surrender anything, give back anything—just come to Him and believe in Him as Savior!"

So they come and believe in the Savior. Later on, in a meeting or conference, they will hear another appeal: "Now that you have received Him as Savior, how would you like to take Him as Lord?"

The fact that we hear this everywhere does not make it right. To urge men and women to believe in a divided Christ is bad teaching, for no one can receive half of Christ, or a third of Christ, or a quarter of the person of Christ! We are not saved by believing in an office nor in a work.

I heard well-meaning workers say, "Come and believe on the finished work." That work will not save you. The Bible does not tell us to believe in an office or a work, but to believe on the Lord Jesus Christ Himself, the person who has done that work and holds those offices.

Now, note again, Peter's emphasis on obedience among the scattered and persecuted Christians of his day. It seems most important to me that Peter speaks of his fellow Christians as "obedient children" (1 Peter 1:14). He was not giving them a command or exhortation to be obedient. In effect, he said, "Assuming that you are believers, I therefore gather that you are also obedient. So now, as obedient children, do so and so."

Brethren, I would point out that obedience is taught throughout the entire Bible and that true obedience is one of the toughest requirements of the Christian life. Apart from obedience, there can be no salvation, for salvation without obedience is a self-contradictory impossibility. The essence of sin is rebellion against divine authority.

God said to Adam and Eve, *"But of the tree of the knowledge of good and evil, thou shalt not eat of it: for in the day that thou eatest thereof thou shalt surely die."* (Gen. 2:17)

Here was a divine requirement calling for obedience on the part of those who had the power of choice and will. In spite of the strong prohibition, Adam and Eve stretched forth their hands and tasted of the fruit and thus they disobeyed and rebelled, bringing sin upon themselves. Paul writes very plainly and directly in the book of Romans about "one man's disobedience" (Rom. 5:19)—and this is a stern word by the Holy Spirit through the apostle—by one man's disobedience came the downfall of the human race!

In John's gospel, the Word is very plain and clear that sin is lawlessness, that sin is disobedience to the law of God. Paul's picture of sinners in Ephesians concludes that the people of the world are "the children of disobedience." (Eph. 2:2) Paul certainly means that disobedience characterizes them, conditions them, molds them. Disobedience has become a part of their nature.

All of this provides background for the great, continuing question before the human race: "Who is boss?" This breaks down into a series of three questions: "To whom do I belong?" "To whom do I owe allegiance?" and "Who has authority to require obedience of me?"

Now, I suppose of all the people in the world Americans have the most difficult time in giving obedience to anyone or anything. Americans are supposed to be sons of freedom. We ourselves were the outcropping of a revolt. We spawned a revolution, pouring the tea overboard in the Boston harbor. We made speeches and said, "That sound of the clash of arms is carried on every wind that blows from the Boston Commons" and finally, "Give me liberty or give me death!"

That is in the American blood, and when anyone says, "You owe obedience," we immediately bristle! In the natural sense, we do not take kindly to the prospect of yielding obedience to anyone. In the same sense, the people of this world have a quick and ready answer to the questions: "To whom do I belong?" and "To whom do I owe obedience?" Their answer is: "I belong to myself. No one has authority to require my obedience!"

A Command and Obligation

Our generation makes a great deal out of this, and we give it the name of "individualism." On the basis of our individuality, we claim the right of self-determination. In an airplane, the pilot who sits at the controls determines where that plane is going. He must determine the destination.

Now, if God had made us humans to be mere machines, we would not have the power of self-determination. But since He made us in His own image and made us to be moral creatures, He has given us that power of self-determination.

The poet Tennyson must have thought about this for he wrote in his "In Memoriam": "Our wills are ours, we know not how; our wills are ours to make them Thine." Oh, this mystery of a man's free will is far too great for us! Tennyson said, "We know not how." But then he girds himself and continues, "Yes, our wills are ours to make them Thine." And that is the only right we have here to make our wills the wills of God, to make the will of God our will!

We must remember that God is Who He is, and we are what we are. God is the Sovereign and we are the creatures. He is the Creator and therefore He has a right to command us with the obligation that we should obey. It is a happy obligation, I might say, for *"[His] yoke is easy, and [His] burden is light."* (Matt. 11:30)

Now, this is where I raise the point again of our human insistence that Christ may sustain a divided relationship toward us. This is now so commonly preached that to oppose it or object to it means that you are sticking your neck out and you had best be prepared for what comes. But how can we insist and teach that our Lord Jesus Christ can be our Savior without being our Lord? How can we continue to teach that we can be saved without any thought of obedience to our Sovereign Lord?

I am satisfied that when man believes on Jesus Christ, he must believe on the whole Lord Jesus Christ—not making any reservation! I am satisfied that it is wrong to look upon Jesus as a kind of divine nurse to whom we can go when sin has made us sick, and after He has helped us, to say goodbye—and go on our own way.

Suppose I slip into a hospital and tell the staff I need a blood transfusion or perhaps an X-ray of my gall bladder. After they have ministered to me and given their services, do I just slip out of the hospital again with a cheery goodbye—as though I owe them nothing and it was kind of them to help me in my time of need? That may sound like a grotesque concept to you, but it does pretty well draw the picture of those who have been taught that they can use Jesus as a Savior in their time of need without owning Him as Sovereign and Lord and without owing Him obedience and allegiance.

The Bible never in any way gives us such a concept of salvation. Nowhere are we ever led to believe that we can use Jesus as a Savior and now own Him as our Lord. He is the Lord and as the Lord He saves us, because He has all of the offices of Savior and Christ and High Priest and Wisdom and Righteousness and Sanctification and Redemption! He is all of these things and all of these are embodied in Him as Christ the Lord.

My brethren, we are not allowed to come to Jesus Christ as shrewd, clever operators saying, "We will take this and this, but we won't take that!" We do not come to Him as one who, buying furniture for his house, declares: "I will take this table but I don't want that chair"— dividing it up! No, sir! It is either all of Christ or none of Christ! I believe we need to preach again a whole Christ to the world—a Christ who does not need our apologies, a Christ who will not be divided, a Christ who will either be Lord of all or who will not be Lord at all!

Sinners Are Fugitives

I think it is important to agree that true salvation restores the right of a Creator-creature relationship because it acknowledges God's right to our fellowship and communion. You see, in our time we have over-emphasized the psychology of the sinner's condition. We spend much time describing the woe of the sinner, the grief of the sinner and the great burden he carries.

He does have all of these, but we have over-emphasized them until we forget the principal fact—that the sinner is actually a rebel against properly constituted authority! That is what makes sin sin. We are rebels. We are sons of disobedience. Sin is the breaking of the law and we are in rebellion and we are fugitives from the just laws of God while we are sinners.

By way of illustration, suppose a man escapes from prison. He will certainly have grief. He is going to be in pain after bumping logs and stones and fences as he crawls and hides away in the dark. He is going to be hungry and cold and weary. His beard will grow long and he will be tired and cramped and cold—all of these will happen, but they are incidental to the fact that he is a fugitive from justice and a rebel against law.

So it is with sinners. They are certainly heartbroken and they carry a heavy load. They certainly labor and are heavy-laden. The Bible takes full account of these things. But they are incidental to the fact that the reason the sinner is what he is, is because he has rebelled against the laws of God and he is a fugitive from divine judgement.

It is that which constitutes the nature of sin; not the fact that he carries a heavy load of misery and sadness and guilt. These things constitute only the outcropping of the sinful nature, but the root of sin is rebellion against God. Does not the sinner say: "I belong to myself—I owe allegiance to no one unless I choose to give it!" That is the essence of sin.

But thankfully, salvation reverses that and restores the former relationship so that the first thing the returning sinner does is to confess: *"Father, I have sinned against heaven, and before thee, and am no more worthy to be called thy son: make me as one of thy hired servants."* (Luke 15:18–19)

Thus, in repentance, we reverse that relationship and we fully submit to the Word of God and the will of God—as obedient children.

Now that happiness of all the moral creatures lies right here, brethren, in the giving of obedience to God. The Psalmist cried out in Psalm 103:21, *"Bless ye the LORD, all ye his hosts; ye ministers of his, that do his pleasure."*

On the other hand, hell is certainly the world of disobedience. Everything else that may be said about hell may be true, but this one thing is the essence—hell is the world of the rebel! Hell is the Alcatraz for the unconstituted rebels who refuse to surrender to the will of God.

I thank God that heaven is the world of God's obedient children. Whatever else we may say of its pearly gates, its golden streets and its jasper walls, heaven is heaven because children of the Most High God find they are in their normal sphere as obedient moral beings. Jesus said there are fire and worms in hell, but that is not the reason it is hell. You might endure worms and fire, but for a moral creature to know and realize that he is where he is because he is a rebel—that is the essence of hell and judgment. It is the eternal world of all the disobedient rebels who have said, "I owe God nothing!"

This is the time given us to decide. Each person makes his own decision as to the eternal world he is going to inhabit.

This is a serious matter of decision. You do not come to this decision as though it were a matter of being interviewed for a job or getting your diploma at a school. We have no basis to believe that we can come casually and sprightly to the Lord Jesus and say, "I have come for some help, Lord Jesus. I understand that You are the Savior so I am going to believe and be saved and then I am going to turn away and think about the other matters of lordship and allegiance and obedience at some time in the future."

I warn you—you will not get help from Him in that way for the Lord will not save those whom He cannot command. He will not divide His offices. You cannot believe on a half-Christ. We take Him for what He is—the anointed Savior and Lord who is King of kings and Lord of lords! He would not be who He is if He saved us and called us and chose us without the understanding that He can also guide and control our lives.

Brethren, I believe in the deeper Christian life and experience—oh, yes! But I believe we are mistaken when we try to add the deeper life to an imperfect salvation, obtained imperfectly by an imperfect concept of the whole thing. Under the working of the Spirit of God through such men as Finney and Wesley, no one would ever dare to rise in a meeting and say, "I am a Christian" if he had not surrendered his whole being to God and had taken Jesus Christ as his Lord. It was only then that he could say, "I am saved!"

Today, we let them say they are saved no matter how imperfect and incomplete the transaction, with the proviso that the deeper Christian life can be tacked on at some time in the future.

Can it be that we really think that we do not owe Jesus Christ our obedience? We have owed Him obedience ever since the second we cried out to Him for salvation, and if we do not give Him that obedience, I have reason to wonder if we are really converted! I see things and I hear of things that Christian people are doing. As I watch them operate within the profession of Christianity I do raise the question of whether they have been truly converted.

Brethren, I believe it is the result of faulty teaching to begin with. They thought of the Lord as a hospital and Jesus as chief of staff to fix up poor sinners that had gotten into trouble!

"Fix me up, Lord," they have insisted, "so that I can go on my own way!"

That is bad teaching, brethren. It is filled with self-deception. Let us look unto Jesus our Lord, high, holy, wearing the crowns, Lord of lords and King of all, having a perfect right to command full obedience from all of His saved people!

8. The Surrender of the Disciple

Our Lord drew a sharp line between the kingdom of God and the world and said that no one could be at the same time a lover of both.

Be Different

The church's mightiest influence is felt when she is different from the world in which she lives. Her power lies in her being different, rises with the degree in which she differs and sinks as the difference diminishes.

This is so fully and clearly taught in the Scriptures and so well illustrated in Church history that it is hard to see how we can miss it. But miss it we do, for we hear constantly that the Church must try to be as much like the world as possible, excepting, of course, where the world is too, too sinful; and we are told to get adjusted to the world and "be all things to all men." (This use of the passage, incidentally, points up Peter's saying that "Our beloved brother Paul" wrote some things which the unlearned and the unstable wrest to their own destruction.)

One sure mark of the Church's heavenly character is that she is different from the rest of mankind; similarity is a mark of her fall. The sons of God and the sons of men are morally and spiritually separated, and between them there is a great gulf fixed. When religious persons try to bridge that gulf by compromise, they violate the very principles of the kingdom of God.

Men are impressed with the message of the Church just as far and as long as she is different from themselves. When she seeks to be like them, they no longer respect her. They believe (and rightly) that she is playing false to herself and to them. The moral jar that results when an indoctrinated son of Adam meets a son of heaven is one of the most wholesome things that can happen to both of them. And contrary to common opinion, men are more inclined to follow the way of Christ when they are compelled to make a radical alteration in their lives than they are when the way is made easy for them.

The human heart senses its need to be changed, and when religion appears offering life without such change, it is not taken seriously by thinking men. The superficial, the insincere, may embrace such a low-powered brand of religion, but the seeking heart must reject it as false and unreal.

All conformity to the world is a negation of our Christian character and a surrender of our heavenly position.

Let us plant ourselves on the hill of Zion and invite the world to come over to us, but never under any circumstances will we go over to them. The cross is the symbol of Christianity, and the cross speaks of death and separation, never of compromise. No one ever compromised with a cross. The cross separated between the dead and the living. The timid and the fearful will cry "Extreme!" and they will be right. The cross is the essence of all that is extreme and final. The message of Christ is a call across a gulf from death to life, from sin to righteousness and from Satan to God.

The first step for any Christian who is seeking spiritual power is to accept his unique position as a son of heaven temporarily detained on the earth, and to begin to live as becometh a saint. The sharp line of demarcation between him and the world will appear at once—and the world will never quite forgive him. And the sons of earth will make him pay well for separation, but it is a price he will gladly pay for the privilege of walking in fruitfulness and power.

The Cross

Crosses are all alike, but no two are identical. Never before nor since has there been a cross experience just like that endured by the Savior. The whole dreadful work of dying which Christ suffered was something unique in the experience of mankind. It had to be so if the cross was to mean life for the world. The sin bearing, the darkness, the rejection by the Father were agonies peculiar to the person of the holy sacrifice. To claim any experience remotely like that of Christ would be more than an error; it would be sacrilege.

Every cross was and is an instrument of death, but no man could die on the cross of another; each man died on his own cross; hence Jesus said, *"Let him ... take up his cross daily, and follow me."* (Luke 9:23, emphasis added)

Now there is a real sense in which the cross of Christ embraces all crosses and the death of Christ encompasses all deaths. *"For the love of Christ constraineth us; because we thus judge, that if one died for all, then were all dead."* (2 Cor. 5:14) *"I am crucified with Christ."* (Gal. 2:20) *"Save in the cross of our Lord Jesus Christ, by whom the world is crucified unto me, and I unto the world."* (6:14)

This is in the judicial working of God in redemption. The Christian as a member of the Body of Christ is crucified along with his divine Head. Before God every true believer is reckoned to have died when Christ died. All subsequent experience of personal crucifixion is based upon this identification with Christ on the cross.

But in the practical, everyday outworking of the believer's crucifixion his own cross is brought into play. "Let him … take up *his* cross daily" (emphasis added). That is obviously not the cross of Christ. Rather, it is the believer's own personal cross by means of which the cross of Christ is made effective in slaying his evil nature and setting him free from its power.

The believer's own cross is one he has assumed voluntarily. Therein lies the difference between his cross and the cross on which Roman convicts died. They went to the cross against their will. He goes because he chooses to do so.

No Roman officer ever pointed to a cross and said, "If any man will, let him." Only Christ said that, and by so saying He placed the whole matter in the hands of the Christian. He can refuse to take his cross, or he can stoop and take it up and start for the dark hill. The difference between great sainthood and spiritual mediocrity depends upon which choice he makes.

To go along with Christ step by step and point by point in identical suffering of Roman crucifixion is not possible for any of us and certainly is not intended by our Lord. What He does intend is that each of us should count himself dead indeed with Christ and then accept willingly whatever of self-denial, repentance, humility, and humble sacrifice that may be found in the path of obedient daily living. That is his cross, and it is the only one the Lord has invited him to bear.

Righteousness

The message to first-century Hebrew Christians was precise and direct: Let Jesus Christ be your motivation to love righteousness and to hate iniquity. In our present century, our spiritual obligations and responsibilities are no different. The character and attributes of Jesus, the eternal Son, have not changed and will not change.

But unto the Son he saith, Thy throne, O God, is for ever and ever: a sceptre of righteousness is the sceptre of thy kingdom. Thou hast loved righteousness, and hated iniquity; therefore God, even thy God, hath anointed thee with the oil of gladness above thy fellows. (Heb. 1:8–9)

When Jesus was on earth, He was not the passive, colorless, spineless person He is sometimes made out to be in paintings and literature. He was a strong man, a man of iron will. He was able to love with an intensity of love that burned Him up. He was able to hate with the strongest degree of hatred against everything that was wrong and evil and selfish and sinful.

Invariably someone will object when I make a statement like that. "I cannot believe such things about Jesus. I always thought it was a sin to hate!" Study long and well the record and the teachings of Jesus while He was on earth. In them lies the answer. It is a sin for the children of God not to hate what ought to be hated. Our Lord Jesus loved righteousness, but He hated iniquity. I think we can say He hated sin and wrong and evil perfectly!

If we are committed, consecrated Christians, truly disciples of the crucified and risen Christ, there are some things we must face. We cannot love honesty without hating dishonesty. We cannot love purity without hating impurity. We cannot love truth without hating lying and deceitfulness.

If we belong to Jesus Christ, we must hate evil even as He hated evil in every form. The ability of Jesus Christ to hate that which was against God and to love that which was full of God was the force that made Him able to receive the anointing—the oil of gladness—in complete measure. On our human side, it is our imperfection in loving the good and hating the evil that prevents us from receiving the Holy Spirit in complete measure. God withholds from us because we are unwilling to follow Jesus in His great poured-out love for what is right and His pure and holy hatred of what is evil.

This question always arises: "Did our Lord Jesus Christ hate sinners?" We already know the answer. He loved the world. We know better than to think that Jesus hated any sinner. Jesus never hated a sinner, but He hated the evil and depravity that controlled the sinner. He did not hate the proud Pharisee, but He detested the pride and self-righteousness of the Pharisee. He did not hate the woman taken in adultery. But he acted against the harlotry that made her what she was.

Jesus hated the devil and He hated those evil spirits that He challenged and drove out. We present-day Christians have been misled and brainwashed, at least in a general way, by a generation of soft, pussycat preachers. They would have us believe that to be good Christians we must be able to purr softly and accept everything that comes along with Christian tolerance and understanding. Such ministers never mention words like *zeal* and *conviction* and *commitment*. They avoid phrases like "standing for the truth."

I am convinced that a committed Christian will show a zealous concern for the cause of Christ. He or she will live daily with a set of spiritual convictions taken from the Bible. He or she will be one of the toughest to move—along with a God-given humility—in his or her stand for Christ.

Why, then, have Christian ministers so largely departed from exhortations to love righteousness with a great, overwhelming love, and to hate iniquity with a deep, compelling revulsion?

People remark how favored the church is in this country. It does not have to face persecution and rejection. If the truth were known, our freedom from persecution is because we have taken the easy, popular way. If we would love righteousness until it became an overpowering passion, if we would renounce everything that is evil, our day of popularity and pleasantness would quickly end. The world would soon turn on us.

We are too nice! We are too tolerant! We are too anxious to be popular! We are too quick to make excuses for sin in its many forms! If I could stir Christians around me to love God and hate sin, even to the point of being a bit of a nuisance, I would rejoice. If some Christian were to call me for counsel saying he or she is being persecuted for

Jesus' sake, I would say with feeling, "Thank God!"

Vance Havner used to remark that too many are running for something when they ought to be standing for something. God's people should be willing to stand! We have become so brainwashed in so many ways that Christians are afraid to speak out against uncleanness in any form. The enemy of our souls has persuaded us that Christianity should be a rather casual thing—certainly not something to get excited about.

Fellow Christian, we have only a little time. We are not going to be here very long. Our triune God demands that we engage in those things that will remain when the world is on fire, for fire determines the value and quality of every person's work.

I have shared these things with you because I am of the opinion that the glad oil, the blessed anointing of the Holy Spirit, is not having opportunity to flow freely among church members of our day. We can hardly expect any such spiritual movement among those who proudly class themselves as liberals. They reject the deity of Christ, the inspiration of the Bible and the divine ministries of the Holy Spirit. How can the oil of God flow among and bless those who do not believe in such an oil of gladness?

But what about us of the evangelical persuasion with our biblical approach to fundamental New Testament truth and teaching? We must ask ourselves why the oil of God is not flowing very noticeably around us. We have the truth. We believe in the anointing and the unction. Why is the oil not flowing?

I think the reason is that we are tolerant of evil. We allow what God hates because we want to be known to the world as good-natured, agreeable Christians. Our stance indicates that the last thing we would want anyone to say about us is that we are narrow-minded. The way to spiritual power and favor with God is to be willing to put away the weak compromises and the tempting evils to which we are prone to cling. There is no Christian victory or blessing if we refuse to turn away from the things that God hates.

Even if your wife loves it, turn away from it.

Even if your husband loves it, turn away from it.

Even if it is accepted in the whole social class and system of which you are a part, turn away from it.

Even if it is something that has come to be accepted by our whole generation, turn away from it if it is evil and wrong and an offense to our holy and righteous Savior.

I am being as frank and as searching as I can possibly be. I know that we lack the courage and the gladness that should mark the committed people of God. And that concerns me. Deep within the human will with which God has endowed us, every Christian holds the key to his or her own spiritual attainment. If he or she will not pay the price of being joyfully led by the Holy Spirit of God, if he or she refuses to hate sin and evil and wrong, our churches might as well be turned into lodges or clubs.

O brother, sister! God has not given up loving us. The Holy Spirit still is God's faithful Spirit. Our Lord Jesus Christ is at the right hand of the Majesty in heaven, representing us there, interceding for us. God is asking us to stand in love and devotion to Him. The day is coming when judgment fire tries every person's work. The hay, wood and stubble of worldly achievement will be consumed. God wants us to know the reward of gold and silver and precious stones.

Following Jesus Christ is serious business. Let us quit being casual about heaven and hell and the judgment to come!

9. The Holiness of the Disciple

Just as he who called you is holy, so be holy in all you do;
for it is written: "Be holy, because I am holy."

1 PETER 1:15–16

You cannot study the Bible diligently and earnestly without being struck by an obvious fact—the whole matter of personal holiness is highly important to God! Neither do you have to give long study to the attitudes of modern Christian believers to discern that, by and large, we consider the expression of true Christian holiness to be just a matter of personal option: "I have looked it over and considered it, but I don't buy it!"

I have always liked the word *exhort* better than *command*, so I remind you that Peter has given every Christian a forceful exhortation to holiness of life and conversation. He clearly bases this exhortation on two great facts—first, the character of God, and second, the command of God.

His argument comes out so simply that we sophisticates stumble over it—God's children ought to be holy because God Himself is holy! We so easily overlook the fact that Peter was an apostle and he is here confronting us with the force of an apostolic injunction, completely in line with the Old Testament truth concerning the person and character of God and also in line with what the Lord Jesus had taught and revealed to His disciples and followers.

Personally, I am of the opinion that we who claim to be apostolic Christians do not have the privilege of ignoring such apostolic injunctions. I do not mean that a pastor can forbid or that a church can compel. I mean only that morally we dare not ignore this commandment: "Be ye holy."

Because it is an apostolic word, we must face up to the fact that we will have to deal with it in some way, and not ignore it—as some Christians do.

Certainly no one has provided us with an option in this matter. Who has ever given us the right or the privilege to look into the Bible and say, "I am willing to consider this matter and if I like it, I will buy it"—using the language of the day.

There is something basically wrong with our Christianity and our spirituality if we can carelessly presume that if we do not like a biblical doctrine and choose not to "buy" it, there is no harm done.

Commandments that we have received from our Lord or from the apostles cannot be overlooked or ignored by earnest and committed Christians. God has never instructed us that we should weigh His desires for us and His commandments to us in the balances of our own judgment and then decide what we want to do about them.

A professing Christian may say, "I have found a place of real Christian freedom; these things just don't apply to me." Of course you can walk out on it! God has given every one of us the power to make our own choices. I am not saying that we are forced to bow our necks to this yoke and we do not have to apply it to ourselves. It is true that if we do not like it, we can turn our backs on it.

The record in the New Testament is plain on this point—many people followed Jesus for a while and then walked away from Him. Once, Jesus said to His disciples: "Except ye eat the flesh of the Son of man, and drink his blood, ye have no life in you." Many looked at one another and then walked away from Him. Jesus turned to those remaining and said, "Will ye also go away?" Peter gave the answer which is still my answer today: "Lord, to whom shall we go? thou hast the words of eternal life" (John 6:53–68).

Those were wise words, indeed, words born of love and devotion.

So, we are not forced to obey in the Christian life, but we are forced to make a choice at many points in our spiritual maturity.

We have that power within us to reject God's instructions—but where else shall we go? If we refuse His words, which way will we turn? If we turn away from the authority of God's Word, to whose authority do we yield? Our mistake is that we generally turn to some other human—a man with breath in his nostrils.

I am old-fashioned about the Word of God and its authority. I am committed to believe that if we ignore it or consider this commandment optional, we jeopardize our souls and earn for ourselves severe judgment to come.

Now, brethren, I have said that the matter of holiness is highly important to God. I have personally counted in an exhaustive concordance and found that the word *holiness* occurs 650 times in the Bible. I have not counted words with a similar meaning in English, such as *sanctify* and *sanctified*, so the count would jump nearer to a thousand if we counted these other words with the same meaning.

This word *holy* is used to describe the character of angels, the nature of heaven and the character of God. It is written that angels are holy and those angels who gaze down upon the scenes of mankind are called the watchers and holy ones.

It is said that heaven is a holy place where no unclean thing can enter in. God Himself is described by the adjective *holy*—Holy Ghost, Holy Lord and Holy Lord God Almighty. These words are used of God throughout the Bible, showing that the highest adjective that can be ascribed to God, the highest attribute that can be ascribed to God is that of holiness, and, in a relative sense, even the angels in heaven partake of the holiness of God.

We note in the Bible, too, that the absence of holiness is given as a reason for not seeing God. I am aware of some of the grotesque interpretations that have been given to the text: "holiness, without which no man shall see the Lord" (Heb. 12:14). My position is this: I will not throw out this Bible text just because some people have misused it to support their own patented theory about holiness. This text does have a meaning and it ought to disturb us until we have discovered what it means and how we may meet its conditions.

What does this word *holiness* really mean? Is it a negative kind of piety from which so many people have shied away? No, of course not! Holiness in the Bible means moral wholeness—a positive quality which actually includes kindness, mercy, purity, moral blamelessness and godliness. It is always to be thought of in a positive, white intensity of degree.

Whenever it is written that God is holy, it means that God is kind, merciful, pure, and blameless in a white, holy intensity of degree. When used of men, it does not mean absolute holiness as it does of God, but it is still the positive intensity of the degree of holiness—and not negative.

This is why true Bible holiness is positive—a holy man can be trusted. A holy man can be tested. People who try to live by a negative standard of piety, a formula that has been copyrighted by other humans, will find that their piety does not stand up in times of difficult testing. Genuine holiness can be put into the place of testing without fear. Whenever there is a breakdown of holiness, that is proof there never was any real degree of holiness in the first place.

Personally, I truly have been affected in my heart by reading the testimonies and commentaries of humble men of God whom I consider to be among the great souls of Christian church history.

I have learned from them that the word and idea of holiness as originally used in the Hebrew did not have first of all the moral connotation. It did not mean that God first of all was pure, for that was taken for granted! The original root of the word *holy* was of something beyond, something strange and mysterious and awe-inspiring. When we consider the holiness of God, we talk about something heavenly, full of awe, mysterious, and fear-inspiring.

Now, this is supreme when it relates to God, but it is also marked in men of God and deepens as men become more like God. It is a sense of awareness of the other world, a mysterious quality and difference that has come to rest upon some men—that is a holiness.

If a man should have that sense and not be morally right, then I would say that he is experiencing a counterfeit of the devil. Whenever Satan has reason to fear a truth very gravely, he produces a counterfeit. He will try to put that truth in such a bad light that the very persons who are most eager to obey it are frightened away from it. Satan is very sly and very experienced in the forming of parodies of truth which he fears the most, and then pawns his parody off as the real thing and soon frightens away the serious-minded saints.

I regret to say that some who have called themselves by a kind of copyrighted name of holiness have allowed the doctrine to harden into a formula that has become a hindrance to repentance, for this doctrine has been invoked to cover up frivolity and covetousness, pride and worldliness. I have seen the results. Serious, honest persons have turned away from the whole idea of holiness because of those who have claimed it and then lived selfish and conceited lives.

But, brethren, we are still under the holy authority of the apostolic command. Men of God have reminded us in the Word that God does ask us and expect us to be holy men and women of God, because we are the children of God, who is holy. The doctrine of holiness may have been badly and often wounded—but the provision of God by His pure and gentle and loving Spirit is still the positive answer for those who hunger and thirst for the life and spirit well-pleasing to God.

When a good man with this special quality and mysterious Presence is morally right and walking in all the holy ways of God and carries upon himself without even knowing it the fragrance of a kingdom that is supreme above the kingdoms of this world, I am ready to accept that as being of God and from God!

By way of illustration, remember that Moses possessed these marks and qualities when he came down from the mount. He had been there with God forty days and forty nights—and when he came back, everyone could tell where he had been. The lightning still played over his countenance, the glory of the Presence remained. This strange something which men cannot pin down or identify was there.

I lament that this mysterious quality of holy Presence has all but forsaken the earth in our day. Theologians long ago referred to it as the numinous, meaning that overplus of something that is more than righteous, but is righteous in a fearful, awe-inspiring, wondrous, heavenly sense. It is as though it is marked with a brightness, glowing with a mysterious fire.

I have commented that this latter quality has all but forsaken the earth and I think the reason is very obvious. We are men who have reduced God to our own terms. In the context of the Christian church, we are now told to "gossip" the gospel and "sell" Jesus to people! We still talk about righteousness, but we are lacking in that bright quality, that numinous that is beyond description.

This mysterious fire was in the bush as you will remember from the Old Testament. A small fire does not frighten people unless it spreads and gets out of control. We are not afraid of fire in that sense, yet we read how Moses, kneeling beside a bush where a small fire burned, hid his face for he was afraid! He had met that mysterious quality. He was full of awe in that manifested Presence.

Later, alone in the mountain and at the sounding of a trumpet, Moses shook, and said, "I exceedingly fear and quake" (Heb. 12:21). We are drawn again and again to that Shekinah that was over Israel for it sums up wonderfully this holiness of God's Presence.

There was the overhanging cloud by day, plainly visible. It was a mysterious cloud not made of water vapor, not casting a shadow anywhere, mysterious. As the light of day would begin to fade, that cloud began to turn incandescent and when the darkness had settled, it shone brightly like one vast light hanging over Israel. Every tent in that diamond-shaped encampment was fully lighted by the strange Shekinah that hung over it.

No man had built that fire. No one added any fuel—no one stoked or controlled it. It was God bringing Himself within the confines of the human eye and shining down in His Presence over Israel.

I can imagine a mother taking her little child by the hand to walk through the encampment. I am sure she would kneel down and whisper to that little fellow: "I want to show you something wonderful. Look! Look at that!"

Probably the response would be: "What is it, Mama?"

Then she would reply in a hushed voice: "That is God—God is there! Our leader Moses saw that fire in the bush. Later, he saw that fire in the mountain. Since we left Egypt that fire of God has followed us and hovered over us all through these years."

"But how do you know it is God, Mama?"

"Because of the Presence in that fire, the mysterious Presence from another world."

This Shekinah, this Presence, had no particular connotation of morality for Israel—that was all taken for granted. It did hold the connotation and meaning of reverence and awe, the solemn and inspiring, different and wonderful and glorious—all of that was there as it was also in the temple.

Then it came down again at Pentecost—that same fire sitting upon each of them—and it rested upon them with an invisible visibility. If there had been cameras, I do not think those tongues of fire could have been photographed—but they were there. It was the sense of being in or surrounded by this holy element, and so strong was it that in Jerusalem when the Christians gathered on Solomon's porch, the people stood off from them as wolves will stand away from a bright camp fire. They looked on, but the Bible says "and of the rest durst no man join himself to them" (Acts 5:13).

Why? Were they held back by any prohibition or restriction? No one had been warned not to come near these praying people, humble and harmless, clean and undefiled. But the crowd could not come. They could not rush in and trample the place down. They stood away from Solomon's porch because they had sensed a holy quality, a mysterious and holy Presence within this company of believers.

Later, when Paul wrote to the Corinthian Christians to explain the mysterious fullness of the Holy Spirit of God, he [basically] said: "Some of you, when you meet together and you hear and obey God, know there is such a sense of God's presence that the unbelievers fall on their faces and then go out and report that God is with you indeed."

Now, that kind of Presence emanates from God as all holiness emanates from God. If we are what we ought to be in Christ and by His Spirit, if the whole sum of our lives beginning with the inner life is becoming more Godlike and Christlike, I believe something of that divine and mysterious quality and Presence will be upon us.

I have met a few of God's saints who appeared to have this holy brightness upon them, but they did not know it because of their humility and gentleness of spirit. I do not hesitate to confess that my fellowship with them has meant more to me than all of the teaching I have ever received. I do stand deeply indebted to every Bible teacher I have had through the years, but they did little but instruct my head. The brethren I have known who had this strange and mysterious quality and awareness of God's Person and Presence instructed my heart.

Do we understand what a gracious thing it is to be able to say of a man, a brother in the Lord, "He is truly a man of God"? He doesn't have to tell us that, but he lives quietly and confidently day by day with the sense of this mysterious, awe-inspiring Presence that comes down on some people and means more than all the glib tongues in the world!

Actually, I am afraid of all the glib tongues. I am afraid of the man who can always flip open his Bible and answer every question—he knows too much! I am afraid of the man who has thought it all out and has a dozen epigrams he can quote, the answers which he has thought up over the years to settle everything spiritual. Brethren, I'm afraid of it! There is a silence that can be more eloquent than all human speech. Sometimes there is a confusion of face and bowing of the head that speaks more divine truth than the most eloquent preacher can impart.

So, Peter reminds us that it is the Lord who has said: "Be ye holy as I am holy, and because I am holy."

First, bring your life into line morally so that God can make it holy; then bring your spiritual life into line that God may settle upon you with the Holy Ghost—with that quality of the Wonderful and the Mysterious and the Divine.

You do not cultivate it and you do not even know it, but it is there and it is this quality of humility invaded by the Presence of God that the church of our day lacks. Oh, that we might yearn for the knowledge and Presence of God in our lives from moment to moment, so that without human cultivation and without toilsome seeking there would come upon us this enduement that gives meaning to our witness! It is a sweet and radiant fragrance and I suggest that in some of our churches it may be strongly sensed and felt.

Now that I have said that, I had better stop and predict that some will ask me, "You don't go by your feelings, do you, Mr. Tozer?" Well, I do not dismiss the matter of feeling and you can quote me on that if it is worth it! Feeling is an organ of knowledge and I do not hesitate to say so. Feeling is an organ of knowledge.

To develop this, will you define the word love for me? I don't believe you can actually define love—you can describe it but you cannot define it. A person or a group of people or a race that has never heard of the word love can never come to an understanding of what love is even if they could memorize the definitions in all of the world's dictionaries.

But just consider what happens to any simple, freckle-faced boy with his big ears and his red hair awry when he first falls in love and the feeling of it comes into every part of his being. All at once, he knows more about love than all of the dictionaries put together!

This is what I am saying—love can only be understood by the feeling of it. The same is true with the warmth of the sun. Tell a man who has no feeling that it is a warm day, and he will never understand what you mean. But take a normal man who is out in the warm sun, and he will soon know it is warm. You can know more about the sun by feeling than you can by description.

So there are qualities in God that can never be explained to the intellect and can only be known by the heart, the innermost being. That is why I say that I do believe in feeling. I believe in what the old writers called religious affection—and we have so little of it because we have not laid the groundwork for it. The groundwork is repentance and obedience and separation and holy living!

I am confident that whenever this groundwork is laid, there will come to us this sense of the other-worldly Presence of God and it will become wonderfully, wonderfully real.

I have at times heard an expression in our prayers, "Oh, God, draw feelingly near!"

I don't think that is too far off—in spite of those who can only draw back and sit in judgment.

"Oh, God, come feelingly near!" God drew feelingly near to Moses in the bush and on the mount. He came feelingly near to the church at Pentecost and He came feelingly near to that Corinthian church when the unbelievers went away awe-struck to report that "God is really in their midst!"

I am willing to confess in humility that we need this in our day.

10.Marks of Discipleship

The Christian Scriptures, particularly the gospel of John, contain two truths that appear to stand opposed to each other. One is that whosoever will may come to Christ. The other is that before anyone can come there must have been a previous work done in his heart by the sovereign operation of God.

The notion that just anybody, at any time, regardless of conditions, can start from religious scratch, without the Spirit's help, and believe savingly on Christ by a sudden decision of the will, is wholly contrary to the teachings of the Bible. God's invitation to men is broad but not unqualified. The word "whosoever" throws the door open wide, indeed, but the church in recent years has carried the gospel invitation far beyond its proper bounds and turned it into something more human and less divine than that found in the sacred Scriptures.

What we tend to overlook is that the word "whosoever" never stands by itself. Always its meaning is modified by the word "believe" or "will" or "come." According to the teachings of Christ no man will or can come and believe unless there has been done within him a prevenient work of God enabling him so to do.

In the sixth chapter of John our Lord makes some statements that gospel Christians seem afraid to talk about. The average one of us manages to live with them by the simple trick of ignoring them. They are such as these:

(1) Only they come to Christ who have been given to Him by the Father (John 6:37).

(2) No one can come of himself; he must first be drawn by the Father (John 6:44).

(3) The ability to come to Christ is a gift of the Father (John 6:65).

(4) Everyone given to the Son by the Father will come to Him (John 6:37).

It is not surprising that upon hearing these words many of our Lord's disciples went back and walked no more with Him. Such teaching cannot but be deeply disturbing to the natural mind. It takes from sinful men much of the power of self-determination upon which they had prided themselves so inordinately. It cuts the ground out from under their self-help and throws them back upon the sovereign good pleasure of God, and that is precisely where they do not want to be. They are willing to be saved by grace, but to preserve their self-esteem they must hold that the desire to be saved originated with them; this desire is their contribution to the whole thing, their offering of the fruit of the ground, and it keeps salvation in their hands where in truth it is not and can never be.

While we admit the difficulties this creates for us, and acknowledge that it runs contrary to the assumptions of popular Christianity, it is yet impossible to deny that there are certain persons who, though still unconverted, are nevertheless different from the crowd, marked out of God, stricken with an interior wound and susceptible to the call of Christ to a degree others are not.

About the teaching as a mere doctrine I am not much concerned, but I am keenly interested in learning how to identify such persons. No man is ever the same after God has laid His hand upon him. He will have certain marks, and though they are not easy to detect perhaps we may cautiously name a few.

One mark is a *deep reverence for divine things*. A sense of the sacred must be present or there can be no receptivity to God and truth. This mysterious feeling of awe precedes repentance and faith and is nothing else but a gift from heaven. Millions go through life unaffected by the presence of God in His world. Good they may be and honest, but they are nevertheless men of earth, "finished and finite clods," and proof against every call of the Spirit.

Another mark is a *great moral sensitivity*. Most persons are apathetic, insensitive to matters of the heart and the conscience, and so are not salvable, at least not in their present condition. But when God begins to work in a man to bring him to salvation, He makes him acutely sensitive to evil. Inward repulsion toward the swine pen that rouses the prodigal and starts him back home is a gift of God to His chosen.

Another mark of the Spirit's working is a *mighty moral discontent*. In spite of our effort to make sinners think they are unhappy the fact is that wherever social and health conditions permit the masses of mankind enjoy themselves very much. Sin has its pleasures (Heb.

11:25) and the vast majority of human beings have a whale of a time living. The conscience is a bit of a pest but most persons manage to strike a truce with it quite early in life and are not troubled much by it thereafter.

It takes a work of God in a man to sour him on the world and to turn him against himself. Yet, until this has happened to him, he is psychologically unable to repent and believe. Any degree of contentment with the world's moral standards or his own lack of holiness successfully blocks off the flow of faith into the man's heart. Esau's fatal flaw was moral complacency; Jacob's only virtue was his bitter discontent.

Again, before a man can be saved, he must feel a *consuming spiritual hunger*. Anyone who lives close to the hearts of men knows that there is little spiritual hunger among them. Religion, pious talk, yes; but not real hunger. Where a hungry heart is found we may be sure that God was there first. *"Ye have not chosen me, but I have chosen you."* (John 15:16)

Cheap Substitutes

In the New Testament salvation and discipleship are so closely related as to be indivisible. They are not identical, but as with Siamese twins they are joined by a tie which can be severed only at the price of death. Yet they are being severed in evangelical circles today. In the working creed of the average Christian salvation is held to be immediate and automatic, while discipleship is thought to be something optional that the Christian may delay indefinitely or never accept at all.

It is not uncommon to hear Christian workers urging seekers to accept Christ now and leave moral and social questions to be decided later. The notion is that obedience and discipleship are unrelated to salvation. We may be saved by believing a historic fact about Jesus Christ—that He died for our sins and rose again—and applying this to our personal situation. The whole biblical concept of lordship and obedience is completely absent from the mind of the seeker. He needs help, and Christ is the very one, even the only one, who can furnish it, so he "takes" Him as his personal Savior. The idea of His lordship is completely ignored.

The absence of the concept of discipleship from present-day Christianity leaves a vacuum that we instinctively try to fill with one or another substitute. I name a few.

Pietism. By this I mean an enjoyable feeling of affection for the person of our Lord that is valued for itself and is wholly unrelated to cross-bearing or the keeping of the commandments of Christ. It is entirely possible to feel for Jesus an ardent love that is not of the Holy Spirit. Witness the love for the Virgin felt by certain devout souls, a love which in the very nature of things must be purely subjective. The heart is adept at emotional tricks and is entirely capable of falling in love with imaginary objects or romantic religious ideas.

In the confused world of romance, young persons are constantly inquiring how they can tell when they are "in love." They are afraid they may mistake some other sensation for true love and are seeking some trustworthy criterion by which they can judge the quality of their latest emotional fever. Their confusion of course arises from the erroneous notion that love is an enjoyable inward passion, without intellectual or volitional qualities and carrying with it no moral obligations.

Our Lord gave us a rule by which we can test our love for Him: "*He that hath my commandments, and keepeth them, he it is that loveth me: and he that loveth me shall be loved of my Father, and I will love him, and will manifest myself to him.... If a man love me, he will keep my words.... He that loveth me not keepeth not my sayings.*" (John 14:21, 23–24)

These words are too plain to need much interpreting. Proof of love for Christ is simply removed altogether from the realm of the feelings and placed in the realm of practical obedience. I think the rest of the New Testament is in full accord with this.

Another substitute for discipleship is *literalism*. Our Lord referred to this when He reproached the Pharisees for their habit of tithing mint and anise and cumin while at the same time omitting the weightier matters of the Law such as justice, mercy and faith. Literalism manifests itself among us in many ways, but it can always be identified in that it lives by the letter of the Word while ignoring its spirit. It habitually fails to apprehend the inward meaning of Christ's words, and contents itself with external compliance with the text.

If Christ commands baptism, for instance, it finds fulfillment in the act of water baptism, but the radical meaning of the act as explained in Romans 6 is completely overlooked. It reads the Scriptures regularly, contributes consistently to religious work, attends church every Sunday and otherwise carries on the common duties of a Christian; and for this it is to be commended. Its tragic breakdown is its failure to comprehend the lordship of Christ, the believer's discipleship, separation from the world and the crucifixion of the natural man.

Literalism attempts to build a holy temple upon the sandy foundation of the religious self. It will suffer, sacrifice and labor, but it will not die. It is Adam at his pious best, but it has never denied self to take up the cross and follow Christ.

Another substitute for discipleship I would mention (though these do not exhaust the list) is *zealous religious activity*. Working for Christ has today been accepted as the ultimate test of godliness among all but a few evangelical Christians. Christ has become a project to be promoted or a cause to be served instead of a Lord to be obeyed. Thousands of mistaken persons seek to do for Christ whatever their fancy suggests should be done, and in whatever way they think best. The what and the how of Christian service can only originate in the sovereign will of our Lord, but the busy beavers among us ignore this fact and think up their own schemes. The result is an army of men who run without being sent and speak without being commanded.

To avoid the snare of unauthorized substitution I recommend a careful and prayerful study of the lordship of Christ and the discipleship of the believer.

11. The Gathering of Disciples

The true Church is a spiritual phenomenon appearing in human society and intermingling with it to some degree but differing from it sharply in certain vital characteristics. It is composed of regenerated persons who differ from other human beings in that they have a superior kind of life imparted to them at the time of their inward renewal.

They are children of God in a sense not true of any other created beings. Their origin is divine and their citizenship is in heaven. They worship God in the Spirit, rejoice in Jesus Christ and have no confidence in the flesh. They constitute a chosen generation, a royal priesthood, a holy nation, a peculiar people.

They have espoused the cause of a rejected and crucified Man Who claimed to be God and Who has pledged His sacred honor that He will prepare a place for them in His Father s house and return again to conduct them there with rejoicing. In the meantime, they carry His cross, suffer whatever indignities men may heap upon them for His sake, act as His ambassadors and do good to all men in His name.

They steadfastly believe that they will share His triumph, and for this reason they are perfectly willing to share His rejection by a society that does not understand them. And they have no hard feelings—only charity and compassion and a strong desire that all men may come to repentance and be reconciled to God. This is a fair summary of one aspect of New Testament teaching about the Church. But another truth more revealing and significant to those seeking information about the gifts of the Spirit is that the Church is a spiritual body, an organic entity united by the life that dwells within it.

The Body, The Head, and the Spirit's Gifts

Each member is joined to the whole by a relationship of life. As a man's soul may be said to be the life of his body, so the indwelling Spirit is the life of the Church.

The idea that the Church is the body of Christ is not an erroneous one, resulting from the pressing too far of a mere figure of speech. The apostle Paul in three of his epistles sets forth this truth in such sobriety of tone and fullness of detail as to preclude the notion that he is employing a casual figure of speech not intended to be taken too literally.

The clear, emphatic teaching of the great apostle is that Christ is the Head of the Church which is His body. The parallel is drawn carefully and continued through long passages. Conclusions are drawn from the doctrine and certain moral conduct is made to depend upon it.

As a normal man consists of a body with various obedient members with a head to direct them, so the true Church is a body, individual Christians being the members and Christ the Head.

The mind works through the members of the body, using them to fulfill its intelligent purposes. Paul speaks of the foot, the hand, the ear, the eye as being members of the body, each with its proper but limited function; but it is the Spirit that worketh in them (1 Cor. 12:1-31).

The teaching that the Church is the body of Christ in 1 Corinthians 12 follows a listing of certain spiritual gifts and reveals the necessity for those gifts.

The intelligent head can work only as it has at its command organs designed for various tasks. It is the mind that sees, but it must have an eye to see through. It is the mind that hears, but it cannot hear without an ear.

And so with all the varied members which are the instruments by means of which the mind moves into the external world to carry out its plans.

As all man's work is done by his mind, so the work of the Church is done by the Spirit, and by Him alone. But to work He must set in the body certain members with abilities specifically created to act as media through which the Spirit can flow toward ordained ends. That in brief is the philosophy of the gifts of the Spirit.

The Concept of Assembly

The church as announced by Christ, seen in the book of Acts and explained by Paul is a thing of great simplicity and rare beauty.

The church as we see it today is unsymmetrical, highly complex and anything but beautiful. Indeed, I think that if some angel of God were made familiar with the church as it appears in the New Testament and then sent to the earth to try to locate it, it would be extremely doubtful whether the heavenly messenger would recognize anything now existing in the field of religion as the church he was looking for. So far have we departed from the pattern shown us in the mount.

The church as the New Testament pictures it is any company of regenerate believers met in the name of Jesus Christ. Such a company is called out from the world and gathered to Christ as a flock of sheep is gathered to the shepherd. The members of this company constitute a despised minority group standing in bold moral contradiction to the world.

Their witness is Christ: His person, work, office and present position at the right hand of the Majesty in the heavens. They carry His gospel to the world and plead "Be ye reconciled to God," then they return to their own company to worship, pray, teach and listen to the Word of the Lord as it is expounded by men of God. They also exhort, testify and exercise for the good of all such spiritual gifts as each one may possess from the Spirit.

Every local church is a microcosm, having all the qualities of the macrocosm, the church universal. Each local company is ideally and should be actually equipped to do anything that the Head of the church wills to accomplish. Wherever such a company is found, there is the true church, the complete church, so complete that if all the believers in the world were to be gathered in one place it would not add anything to the perfection of the smaller assembly.

Each local church is a fellowship in the deepest spiritual meaning of that word. It comes into being by an afflatus of power and a bestowment of life. It cannot be produced by organization, though after it is there, it may be strengthened and improved by a wise and Spirit-led organization.

A true church existed in Crete before Titus was left there to "set in order the things that are wanting, and ordain elders in every city." Organization did not create the church; it was imposed upon a church already present, a church which had been born out of the preaching of the gospel. For it is always the gospel that produces the church; there can be no church apart from the gospel.

Leaving out of consideration other problems and other times we'll look briefly at two forces that have worked to destroy the assembly concept in this generation:

The first is denominationalism, the dividing of believing men into mutually exclusive camps. This is not peculiar to these times, but we today are reaping the fruit of a tree planted long ago. Though I have for many years worked in a denomination and preached freely among other denominations I am not blind to the mischief that accompanies this extra-scriptural phenomenon.

I do not here offer a remedy for denominationalism. I merely report the facts, and they are not encouraging. To enter any place of worship where the saints of God meet conscious of denominational loyalties or hostilities is to lose completely the sense of communion with Christ and each other so vital to true worship. I believe a few individual saints may be godly enough to escape the trap, but I am sure the larger numbers are not.

Another force that has helped to block out the New Testament concept of the church is tabernacleism. This phenomenon flourished during the second and third decade of this century, and though it has passed it has unfortunately left behind it the religious philosophy that brought it into being, as well as the spirit and mood it created.

Tabernacleism, oddly enough, came as a revolt from denominationalism. Certain gifted men got their fill of ecclesiastical machinery and broke away to start independent religious groups made up of others like themselves. Often with but a modicum of theological knowledge and with no time nor inclination to learn, they turned to the theater for their technique. And it worked, surprisingly, astonishingly well.

The concept of the church held by the founders and promoters of tabernacleism may be learned easily enough by noticing the nomenclature that accompanied it: "work" instead of assembly or church; "program" instead of worship; "artist" (used for any fifth-rate performer on the handsaw or consecrated cowbells); "talent" (to refer to a performer); "one night appearance," "in person" (borrowed from the theater), and many other such terms, unconscious confessions that the saints had left the ways of God and gone in the ways of fallen men. And this while making the strongest protestations of orthodoxy.

I do not mean to scold, and I am grateful for any shreds of New Testament worship that may be left among us; but I cannot but hope and pray that the evangelical church may soon return to the land of promise. We have been in Babylon long enough. And one of the first things she must rediscover before she comes home is her own identity.

Without doubt the most important body on earth is the Church of God which He purchased with His own blood.

Unfortunately, the word "church" itself has taken on meanings which it did not originally have and has suffered untold injury in the house both of its enemies and of its friends.

The meaning of the word for the true Christian was fixed by our Lord and His apostles. What they meant by it is what we must mean by it; and no man and no angel has authority to change it.

The simple etymological meaning is easy to discover, but its larger significance must be learned from the New Testament Scriptures. All that is meant by that wondrous word cannot be stated in one sentence, nor in one paragraph, nor scarcely in one book.

The universal Church is the body of Christ, the bride of the Lamb, the habitation of God through the Spirit, the pillar and ground of the truth.

The local church is a community of ransomed men, a minority group, a colony of heavenly souls dwelling apart on the earth, a division of soldiers on a foreign soil, a band of reapers, working under the direction of the Lord of the harvest, a flock of sheep following the Good Shepherd, a brotherhood of like-minded men, a visible representative of the Invisible God.

It is most undesirable to conceive of our churches as "Works," or "Projects." If such words must be used, then let them be understood as referring to the earthly and legal aspect of things only. A true church is something supernatural and divine, and is in direct lineal descent from that first church at Jerusalem. Insofar as it is a church it is spiritual; its social aspect is secondary and may be imitated by any group regardless of its religious qualities or lack of them. The spiritual essence of a true church cannot be reproduced anywhere but in a company of renewed and inwardly united believers.

The Christian life begins with the individual; a soul has a saving encounter with God and the new life is born. Not all the pooled efforts of any church can make a Christian out of a lost man. But once the "great transaction's done" the communion of believers will be found to be the best environment for the new life. Men are made for each other, and this is never more apparent than in the church.

All else being equal, the individual Christian will find in the communion of a local church the most perfect atmosphere for the fullest development of his spiritual life. There also he will find the best arena for the largest exercise of those gifts and powers with which God may have endowed him.

The religious solitary may gain on a few points, and he may escape some of the irritations of the crowd, but he is a half-man, nevertheless, and worse, he is a half-Christian. Every solitary experience, if we would realize its beneficial effects, should be followed immediately by a return to our own company. There will be found the faith of Christ in its most perfect present manifestation.

But one thing must be kept in mind: these things are true only where the local church is a church indeed, where the communion of saints is more than a phrase from the Creed but is realized and practiced in faith and love. Those religio-social institutions, with which we are all too familiar, where worship is a form, the sermon an essay and the prayer an embarrassed address to someone who isn't there, certainly do not qualify as churches under any scriptural terms with which we are acquainted.

The elements of a true church are few and easy to possess. They are a company of believers, the Lord, the Spirit and the Word of the Living God. Let the Lord be worshiped, the Spirit be obeyed, the Word be expounded and followed as the only rule for faith and conduct, and the power of God will begin to show itself as it did to Samson in the camp of Dan.

The church will produce a spiritual culture all its own, wholly unlike anything created by the mind of man and superior to any culture known on earth, ancient or modern. God is getting His people ready for another world, and He uses the local church as a workshop in which to carry on His blessed work.

That Christian is a happy one who has found a company of true believers in whose heavenly fellowship he can live and love and labor. And nothing else on earth should be as dear to him nor command from him such a degree of loyalty and devotion.

The Church Cannot Die

There is a notion abroad that Christianity is on its last legs, or possibly already dead and just too weak to lie down.

This is confidently believed in Communist countries, and while spokesmen for the West are too polite to say so, one can hardly escape the feeling that they too believe the demise of the church to be a certain if embarrassing fact, the chief proof of her death being her failure to provide leadership for the world just when it needs it most.

Let me employ a pair of mixed and battered but still useful clichés and say that those who have come to bury the faith of our fathers have reckoned without the host. Just as Jesus Christ was once buried away with the full expectation that He had been gotten rid of, so His church has been laid to rest times without number. And as He disconcerted His enemies by rising from the dead so the church has confounded hers by springing again to vigorous life after all the obsequies had been performed over her coffin and the crocodile tears had been shed at her grave.

The language of devotion has helped to create the impression that the church is supposed to be a band of warriors driving the enemy before them in plain sight and with plenty of colour and drama to give a pleasing flourish to the whole thing. In our hymns and pulpit oratory we have commonly pictured the church as marching along to the sound of martial music and the plaudits of the multitude.

Of course, this is but a poetic figure. The individual Christian may be likened to a soldier, but the picture of the church on earth as a conquering army is not realistic. Her true situation is more accurately portrayed as a flock of sheep in the midst of wolves, or as a company of despised pilgrims plodding toward home, or as a peculiar nation protected by the Passover blood waiting for the sound of the trumpet, or as a bride looking for the coming of her bridegroom.

The world is constantly lashing the church because she has no solution for the problems of society, and the religious leaders who do not know the score wince under the lash. Every once in a while, some churchman in an acute attack of conscience does penance in public for Christianity's failure to furnish bold leadership for the world in this time of crisis. "We have sinned," cries the frustrated prophet. "The world looked to us for help and we have failed it."

Well, I am all for repentance if it is genuine, and I think the church has failed, not by neglecting to provide leadership but by living too much like the world. That, however, is not what the muddled churchman means when he bares his soul in public. Rather, he erroneously assumes that the church of God has been left on earth to minister good hope and cheer to the world in such quantities that it can ignore God, reject Christ, glorify fallen human flesh and pursue its selfish ends in peace. The world wants the church to add a dainty spiritual touch to its carnal schemes, and to be there to help it to its feet and put it to bed when it comes home drunk with fleshly pleasures.

In the first place the church has received no such commission from her Lord, and in the second place the world has never shown much disposition to listen to the church when she speaks in her true prophetic voice. The attitude of the world toward the true child of God is precisely the same as that of the citizens of Vanity Fair toward Christian and his companion. "Therefore they took them and beat them, and besmeared them with dirt, and put them into the cage, that they might be made a spectacle to all men." Christian's duty was not to "provide leadership" for Vanity Fair but to keep clean from its pollution and get out of it as fast as possible. He that hath ears to hear, let him hear.

Christianity is going the way her Founder and His apostles said it would go. Its development and direction were predicted almost two thousand years ago, and this itself is a miracle. Had Christ been less than God and His apostles less than inspired, they could not have foretold with such precision the state of the church so far removed from them in time and circumstance.

No mortal man could have foreseen the coming of the great religio-political system that is Rome, or the Dark Ages, or the discovery of the New World, or the Industrial Revolution and the rise of higher criticism, or the nuclear age, and man's adventure into space. All these would have upset any human effort to foretell the religious situation these latter days; but present conditions were in fact depicted in great fullness of detail nearly two thousand years ago. Nothing unexpected has happened or is happening.

We are in real need of a reformation that will lead to revival among the churches, but the church is not dead, neither is it dying. The church cannot die.

A local church can die. This happens when all the old saints in a given place fall asleep and no young saints arise to take their place. Sometimes under these circumstances the congregation ceases to be a church, or there is no congregation left and the doors of the chapel are nailed shut. But such a condition, however deplorable, should not discourage us. The true church is the repository of the life of God among men, and if in one place the frail vessels fail, that life will break out somewhere else.

Of this we may be sure.

12. The Voice of the Disciple

An Urge to Share

Spiritual experiences must be shared. It is not possible for very long to enjoy them alone. The very attempt to do so will destroy them.

The reason for this is obvious. The nearer our souls draw to God the larger our love will grow. And the greater our love, the more unselfish we shall become, and the greater our care for the souls of others. Hence increased spiritual experience, so far as it is genuine, brings with it a strong desire that others may know the same grace that we ourselves enjoy. This leads quite naturally to an increased effort to lead others to a closer and more satisfying fellowship with God.

The human race is one. God "made of one blood all nations of men for to dwell on all the face of the earth," and He made the individual members of society for each other. Not the hermit but the man in the midst of society is in the best place to fulfill the purpose for which he was created. There may be circumstances when for a time it will be necessary for the seeker after God to wrestle alone like Jacob on the bank of the river, but the result of his lonely experience is sure to flow out to family and friend, and on out to society at last. In the nature of things, it must be so.

The impulse to share, to impart, normally accompanies any true encounter with God and spiritual things. The woman at the well, after her soul-inspiring meeting with Jesus, left her waterpots, hurried into the city and tried to persuade her friends to come out and meet Him. "Come, see a man," she said, "which told me all things that ever I did: is not this the Christ?" Her spiritual excitement could not be contained within her own heart. She had to tell someone.

Is it not possible that our Lord had this in mind when He spoke about the impossibility of secret discipleship? Have we misunderstood the true relationship between faith and testimony? Christ made it clear that there could be no such thing as secret discipleship and Paul said, *"With the heart man believeth unto righteousness; and with the mouth confession is made unto salvation."*

This is usually understood to mean that God has laid upon us an arbitrary requirement to open our mouth in confession before salvation can become effective within us. Maybe that is the correct meaning of these verses. Or could it be that the confession is evidence of the salvation which has come by faith to the heart, and where there is no impulse to impart, no outrushing of words in joyous testimony, there has been no true inward experience of saving grace?

The irrepressible urge to share spiritual blessings can explain a great many religious phenomena. It even goes so far as to create a kind of vicarious transfer of interest from one person to another, so that the blessed soul would, if necessary, give up its own blessing that another might receive. Only thus can that prayer of Moses be understood, *"Oh, this people have sinned a great sin, and have made them gods of gold. Yet now, if thou wilt forgive their sin—; and if not, blot me, I pray thee, out of thy book which thou hast written."* (Exodus 32:31, 32)

His great care for Israel had made him incautious, almost rash, before the Lord in their behalf. Moses felt that for Israel to be forgiven was reward enough for him. This impulsive uprush of vicarious love can hardly be defended before the bar of pure reason. But God understood and complied with Moses' request.

The intense urge to have others enjoy the same spiritual privileges as himself once led Paul to make a statement so extreme, so reckless, that reason cannot approve it; only love can understand: *"I say the truth in Christ, I lie not, my conscience also bearing me witness in the Holy Ghost, that I have great heaviness and continual sorrow in my heart. For I could wish that myself were accursed from Christ for my brethren, my kinsmen according to the flesh."* (Romans 9:1-3)

In the light of this, it is quite easy to understand why all great Christian teachers have insisted that true spiritual experience must be shared. The careless person who remarks that he does not need to go to church to serve God is far from understanding the most elementary spiritual truths. By cutting himself off from the religious community he proves that he has never felt the deep urge to share—and for the very reason that he has nothing to share. He has never felt the constraining love of Christ, so he can go his way in silence. His withdrawal from the believing fellowship tells us more about him than he knows about himself.

"Being let go, they went to their own company." So it was in the Early Church and so it has always been when men meet God in saving encounter. They want to share the blessed benefits.

Moral Implications of the Gospel

To many observing persons today, it appears that conversion does not do for people as much as it once did. Too often the experience passes, leaving the seeker unsatisfied and deeply disappointed. Some who are thus affected, and who are too sincere to play with religion, walk out on the whole thing and turn back frankly to the old life. Others try to make what they can out of a bad bargain and gradually adjust themselves to a modified and imperfect form of Christianity spiced up with synthetic fun and enlivened by frequent shots of stimulants in the form of "gimmicks," to give it relish and sparkle.

The knowledge that revival campaigns can come and go without raising the moral level of the cities and towns where they are held should surely give us serious pause. Something is wrong somewhere. Could it be that the cause back of this undeniable failure of the gospel to effect moral change is a further-back failure of the messenger to grasp the real meaning of his message? Could it be that, in his eagerness to gain one more convert, he makes the Way of Life too easy? It would seem so.

In other times, it was not an uncommon thing to witness the wholesale closing of saloons and brothels as a direct result of the preaching of the message of Christ in revival campaigns. Surely there must have been a difference of emphasis between the message they preached in those days and the ineffective message we preach today.

To allow the gospel only its etymological meaning of good news is to restrict it so radically as actually to make it something it is not. That "Christ died for our sins according to the scriptures" is good news indeed. That He, having by Himself purged our sins, sat down on the right hand of the Majesty in the heavens from which exalted position He mediates grace to all believers, is wonderful, heartening news for the sin burdened race. But to limit the Christian message to this one truth alone is to rob it of much of its meaning and create a bad misunderstanding among those who hear the resultant preaching.

The fact is that the New Testament message embraces a great deal more than an offer of free pardon. It is a message of pardon, and for that may God be praised; but it is also a message of repentance. It is a message of atonement, but it is also a message of temperance and righteousness and godliness in this present world. It tells us that we must accept a Savior, but it tells us also that we must deny ungodliness and worldly lusts. The gospel message includes the idea of amendment, of separation from the world, of cross-carrying and loyalty to the kingdom of God even unto death.

To be strictly technical, these latter truths are corollaries of the gospel, and not the gospel itself; but they are part and parcel of the total message which we are commissioned to declare. No man has authority to divide the truth and preach only a part of it. To do so is to weaken it and render it without effect.

This is more than a mere splitting of definitions. It has real consequences among Christian workers and, what is more serious, it has consequences among the trusting seekers who come to these workers for counsel. To offer a sinner the gift of salvation based upon the work of Christ, while at the same time allowing him to retain the idea that the gift carries with it no moral implications, is to do him untold injury where it hurts him worst.

Many evangelical teachers insist so strongly upon free, unconditional grace as to create the impression that sin is not a serious matter and that God cares very little about it. He is concerned only with our escaping the consequences. The gospel then, in practical application, means little more than a way to escape the fruits of our past.

The heart that has felt the weight of its own sin and along with this has seen the dread whiteness of the Most High God will never believe that a message of forgiveness without transformation is a message of good news. To remit a man's past without transforming his present is to violate the moral sincerity of his own heart. To that kind of thing God will be no party.

We must have courage to preach the whole message. By so doing we shall undoubtedly lose a few friends and make a number of enemies. But the true Christian will not grieve too much about that. He has enough to do to please his Lord and Savior and to be true to the souls of all men. That may well occupy him too completely to leave much time for regrets over the displeasure of misguided men.

13. The End of the Disciple

For he was looking forward to the city with foundations, whose architect and builder is God.

HEBREWS 11:10

No More Watchfulness

A short generation ago, or about the time of the first World War, there was a feeling among gospel Christians that the end of the age was near, and many were breathless with anticipation of a new world order about to emerge.

This new order was to be preceded by a silent return of Christ to earth, not to remain, but to raise the righteous dead to immortality and to glorify the living saints in the twinkling of an eye. These He would catch away to the marriage supper of the Lamb, while the earth meanwhile plunged into its baptism of fire and blood in the Great Tribulation. This would be relatively brief, ending dramatically with the battle of Armageddon and the triumphant return of Christ with His Bride to reign a thousand years.

Thus, the hopes and dreams of Christians were directed toward an event to be followed by a new order in which they would have a leading part. This expectation for many was so real that it quite literally determined their world outlook and way of life.

One well-known and highly respected Christian leader, when handed a sum of money to pay off the mortgage on the church building, refused to use it for that purpose. Instead, he used it to help send missionaries to the heathen to hasten the Lord's return. This is probably an extreme example, but it does reveal the acute apocalyptic expectation that prevailed among Christians around the time of World War I and immediately following.

Before we condemn this as extravagant, we should back off a bit and try to see the whole thing in perspective. We may be wiser now (though that is open to serious question), but those Christians had something very wonderful which we today lack.

They had a unifying hope; we have none. Their activities were concentrated; ours are scattered, overlapping and often self-defeating. They fully expected to win; we are not even sure we know what "win" means. Our Christian hope has been subjected to so much examination, analysis and revision that we are embarrassed to admit that we have such a hope at all.

And those expectant believers were not wholly wrong. They were only wrong about the time. They saw Christ's triumph as being nearer than it was, and for that reason their timing was off; but their hope itself was valid. Many of us have had the experience of misjudging the distance of a mountain toward which we were travelling.

The huge bulk that loomed against the sky seemed very near, and it was hard to persuade ourselves that it was not receding as we approached. So the City of God appears so large to the minds of the world-weary pilgrim that he is sometimes the innocent victim of an optical illusion; and he may be more than a little disappointed when the glory seems to move farther away as he approaches.

But the mountain is there; the traveler need only press on to reach it. And the Christian's hope is there too; his judgment is not always too sharp, but he is not mistaken in the long view; he will see the glory in God's own time.

We evangelicals have become sophisticated, blasé. We have lost what someone called the "millennial component" from our Christian faith. To escape what we believe to be the slough of a mistaken hope we have detoured far out into the wilderness of complete hopelessness.

Christians now chatter learnedly about things simple believers have always taken for granted. They are on the defensive, trying to prove things that a previous generation never doubted. We have allowed unbelievers to get us in a corner and have given them the advantage by permitting them to choose the time and place of encounter. We smart under the attack of the quasi-Christian unbeliever, and the nervous, self-conscious defense we make is called "the religious dialogue."

Under the scornful attack of the religious critic real Christians who ought to know better are now "rethinking" their faith. Scarcely anything has escaped the analysts.

With a Freudian microscope they examine everything: foreign missions, the Book of Genesis. the inspiration of the Scriptures, morals, all tried and proven methods, polygamy, liquor, sex, prayer - all have come in for inquisition by those who engage in the contemporary dialogue. Adoration has given way to celebration in the holy place, if indeed any holy place remains to this generation of confused Christians.

Cause of Declining Expectation

The causes of the decline of apocalyptic expectation are many, not the least being the affluent society in which we live. If the rich man with difficulty enters the kingdom of God, then it would be logical to conclude that a society having the highest percentage of well-to-do persons in it would have the lowest percentage of Christians, all things else being equal. If the "deceitfulness of riches" chokes the Word and makes it unfruitful, then this would be the day of near-fruitless preaching, at least in the opulent West.

And if surfeiting and drunkenness and worldly cares tend to unfit the Christian for the coming of Christ, then this generation of Christians should be the least prepared for that event.

On the North American continent Christianity has become the religion of the prosperous middle and upper classes almost entirely, the very rich or the very poor rarely become practicing Christians. The touching picture of the poorly dressed, hungry saint, clutching his Bible under his arm and with the light of God shining in his face hobbling painfully toward the church, is chiefly imaginary. One of the biggest problems of even the most ardent Christian these days is to find a parking place for the shiny chariot that transports him effortlessly to the house of God where he hopes to prepare his soul for the world to come.

In the United States and Canada, the middle class today possesses more earthly goods and lives in greater luxury than emperors and maharajas did a short century ago. And since the bulk of Christians comes from this class it is not difficult to see why the apocalyptic hope has all but disappeared from among us. It is hard to focus attention upon a better world to come when a more comfortable one than this can hardly be imagined. The best we can do is to look for heaven after we have reveled for a lifetime in the luxuries of a fabulously generous earth. As long as science can make us so cozy in this present world it is hard to work up much pleasurable anticipation of a new world order.

But affluence is only one cause of the decline of the apocalyptic hope. There are other and more important ones.

The whole problem is a big one, a theological one, a moral one. An inadequate view of Christ may be the chief trouble. Christ has been explained, humanized, demoted. Many professed Christians no longer expect Him to usher in a new order; they are not at all sure that He is able to do so; or if He does, it will be with the help of art, education, science and technology; that is, with the help of man. This revised expectation amounts to disillusionment for many. And of course no one can become too radiantly happy over a King of kings who has been stripped of His crown or a Lord of lords who has lost His sovereignty.

Another cause of the decline of expectation is hope deferred which, according to the proverb, *"maketh the heart sick."* The modern civilised man is impatient; he takes the short-range view of things. He is surrounded by gadgets that get things done in a hurry.

He was brought up on quick oats; he likes his instant coffee; he wears drip-dry shirts and takes one-minute Polaroid snapshots of his children. His wife shops for her spring hat before the leaves are down in the fall. His new car, if he buys it after June 1, is already an old model when he brings it home. He is almost always in a hurry and can't bear to wait for anything.

This breathless way of living naturally makes for a mentality impatient of delay, and when this man enters the kingdom of God he brings his short-range psychology with him. He finds prophecy too slow for him. His first radiant expectations soon lose their luster. He is likely to inquire, *"Lord, wilt thou at this time restore again the kingdom to Israel?"* and when there is no immediate response he may conclude, "My lord delayeth his coming." The faith of Christ offers no buttons to push for quick service.

The new order must wait the Lord's own time, and that is too much for the man in a hurry. He just gives up and becomes interested in something else.

Another cause is eschatological confusion. The vitalising hope of the emergence of a new world wherein dwelleth righteousness be-

came an early casualty in the war of conflicting prophetic interpretations. Teachers of prophecy, who knew more than the prophets they
claimed to teach, debated the fine points of Scripture ad infinitum
while a discouraged and disillusioned Christian public shook their
heads and wondered. A leader of one evangelical group told me that
his denomination had recently been, in his words, "split down the
middle" over a certain small point of prophetic teaching, one incidentally which had never been heard of among the children of God until
about one hundred years ago.

Certain popular views of prophecy have been discredited by events
within the lifetime of some of us; a new generation of Christians
cannot be blamed if their Messianic expectations are somewhat confused. When the teachers are divided, what can the pupils do?

It should be noted that there is a vast difference between the doctrine
of Christ's coming and the hope of His coming. The first we may hold
without feeling a trace of the second. Indeed, there are multitudes of
Christians today who hold the doctrine of the second coming. What
I have talked about here is that overwhelming sense of anticipation
that lifts the life onto a new plane and fills the heart with rapturous
optimism. This is what we today lack.

Frankly, I do not know whether or not it is possible to recapture the
spirit of anticipation that animated the Early Church and cheered the
hearts of gospel Christians only a few decades ago. Certainly scold-
ing will not bring it back, nor arguing over prophecy, nor condemn-
ing those who do not agree with us. We may do all or any of these
things without arousing the desired spirit of joyous expectation.

That unifying, healing, purifying hope is for the childlike, the inno-
cent-hearted, the unsophisticated.

Possibly nothing short of a world catastrophe that will destroy every
false trust and turn our eyes once more upon the Man Christ Jesus
will bring back the glorious hope to a generation that has lost it.

The Trumpet Will Sound

I have found there is an entirely new way to shock complacent Christians in our churches today. These Christians go into shock when I
say that it is an error to assume that being saved is to be automatically

ready for heaven. Very few people in our churches are willing to consider what the Bible actually teaches about discipline and chastening in preparing us for our heavenly home. The writer of the letter to the Hebrews gave definite instruction to those who were children of God through faith in our Lord Jesus Christ:

If ye endure chastening, God dealeth with you as with sons; for what son is he whom the father chasteneth not? But if ye be without chastisement, whereof all are partakers, then are ye bastards, and not sons.... He [chastens us] for our profit, that we might be partakers of his holiness.... Follow peace with all men, and holiness, without which no man shall see the Lord. (Heb. 12:7–14)

Now, I know I will have to explain what I mean about our daily Christian lives being in preparation for an eternity in the heavenly realms. First, let us see if we are in agreement about the most important proclamation that we can make concerning faith.

There is no doubt about it. First in importance concerning faith is the good news—the truth that every man and woman in our lost world may have God's gifts of forgiveness and eternal life through believing faith in Jesus Christ as Savior and Lord. It is not possible to overstate the importance of this basic truth in the Christian gospel. It has been proclaimed often. Paul gave this stark, simple instruction concerning salvation to the jailer at Philippi: "*Believe on the Lord Jesus Christ, and thou shalt be saved, and thy house.*" (Acts 16:31)

As Christian believers (I am assuming you are a believer), you and I know how we have been changed and regenerated and assured of eternal life by faith in Jesus Christ and His atoning death. On the other hand, where this good news of salvation by faith is not known, religion becomes an actual bondage. If Christianity is known only as a religious institution, it may well become merely a legalistic system of religion, and the hope of eternal life becomes a delusion.

I have said this much about the reality and assurance of our salvation through Jesus Christ in order to counter the shock you may feel when I add that God wants to fully prepare you in your daily Christian life so that you will be ready indeed for heaven. Perhaps it is a good thing for you if you are shocked. It is my observation that many Christians are so cosmopolitan, so worldly wise, so self-assured that they are past being shocked by anything!

Probably your first question as you come out of shock will be, "Have you forgotten the dying thief? Did not our Lord tell him his faith had made him ready for paradise?"

Let me share something with you. No one could love the Christian gospel and witness it to others without an understanding that the God of all grace has surely made a necessary provision for those who may trust Jesus in the final hours of life. We admit our humanness. We do not have God's wisdom and discernment. Only God is all-knowing and all-powerful. He is full of grace and truth. We can trust Him to be faithful and right in all of His dealings with us.

Remember that most believers have been found of the Lord and received His love and grace at an earlier time in their lives. Many testify to faith extending back to their childhood. Thus, they have been in God's household for a long time, and He has been trying to do something special within their beings day after day, year after year. His purpose has been to bring many sons—and daughters, too—to glory.

Now, if we are truly sons and daughters by faith, we will respond to the wise discipline and the necessary rebukes aimed at bringing us to the full measure of spiritual stature. God's motives are loving. Our heavenly Father disciplines us for our own good, *"that we might be partakers of his holiness"* (Heb. 12:10).

I have known people who seemed to be terrified by God's loving desire that we should reflect His own holiness and goodness. As God's faithful children, we should be attracted to holiness, for holiness is God-likeness—likeness to God!

God encourages every Christian believer to follow after holiness. Holiness is to be our constant ambition—not as holy as God is holy, but holy because God is holy. We know who we are and God knows who He is. He does not ask us to be God, and He does not ask us to produce the holiness that only He Himself knows. Only God is holy absolutely; all other beings can be holy only in relative degrees.

The angels in heaven do not possess God's holiness. They are created beings and they are contented to reflect the glory of God. That is their holiness.

Holiness is not terrifying. Actually, it is amazing and wonderful that God should promise us the privilege of sharing in His nature. It is impossible for any person to be as holy as God is holy. It is encouraging that God "knoweth our frame" (Ps. 103:14). He remembers we were made of dust. So He tells us what is in His being as He thinks of us: "Be holy because I am your God and I am holy! It is My desire that you grow in grace and in the knowledge of Me. I want you to be more like Jesus, My eternal Son, every day you live!"

Our Lord endeavors to prepare us for our eternal fellowship with the saints, the martyrs, the heroes of the faith who suffered through fire and flood and blood and tears when they were God's pilgrims on this earth. Do not try to short-circuit God's plans for your discipleship and spiritual maturing here. If you and I were already prepared for heaven in that moment of our conversion, God would have taken us there instantly!

As believers and disciples, we are satisfied to know that the mysterious quality of God's holy person sets Him apart from all others and all else throughout His entire universe. God exists in Himself. His holy nature is such that we cannot comprehend Him with our minds.

God's holy nature is unique. He is of a substance not shared by any other being. Hence, God can be known only as He reveals Himself. There is absolutely no other way for us to know Him.

In Old Testament times, whenever this utterly holy God revealed Himself in some way to mankind, terror and amazement were the reaction. People saw themselves as guilty and unclean by contrast.

Early in the Revelation, the final book of the Bible, the apostle John describes the overwhelming nature of his encounter with the Lord of glory. He says, *"And when I saw him, I fell at his feet as dead"* (Rev. 1:17). John was a man, a person born into a sinful world. But he was a believer and an apostle. At the time, he was in exile *"for the word of God, and for the testimony of Jesus Christ"* (1:9). But when the risen, glorified Lord Jesus appeared to him on Patmos, John sank down in abject humility and fear.

Jesus at once reassured him, stooping to place a nail-pierced hand on the prostrate apostle. "Fear not," Jesus said to John. *"I am the first and the last: I am he that liveth, and was dead; and, behold, I am alive for evermore, Amen; and have the keys of hell and of death"* (1:17–18). Then Jesus proceeded to give His apostle a writing assignment: *"Write the things which thou hast seen, and the things which are, and the things which shall be hereafter"* (1:19).

I notice particularly that the Lord did not condemn John. He knew that John's weakness was the reaction to revealed divine strength. He knew that John's sense of unworthiness was the instant reaction to absolute holiness. Along with John, every redeemed human being needs the humility of spirit that can only be brought about by the manifest presence of God.

This mysterious yet gracious Presence is the air of life eternal. It is the music of existence, the poetry of the Christian life. It is the beauty and wonder of being one of Christ's own—a sinner born again, regenerated, created anew to bring glory to God. To know this Presence is the most desirable state imaginable for anyone. To live surrounded by this sense of God is not only beautiful and desirable, but it is also imperative!

Know that our living Lord is unspeakably pure. He is sinless, spotless, immaculate, stainless. In His person is an absolute fullness of purity that our words can never express. This fact alone changes our entire human and moral situation and outlook. We can always be sure of the most important of all positives: God is God and God is right. He is in control. Because He is God He will never change!

I repeat: God is right—always. That statement is the basis of all we are thinking about God.

When the eternal God Himself invites us to prepare ourselves to be with Him throughout the future ages, we can only bow in delight and gratitude, murmuring, "Oh, Lord, may Your will be done in this poor, unworthy life!"

I can only hope that you are wise enough, desirous enough and spiritual enough to face up to the truth that every day is another day of spiritual preparation, another day of testing and discipline with our heavenly destination in mind. For as I hope you have already seen, full qualification for eternity is not instant or automatic or painless.

I hope, too, that you may begin to understand in this context why our evangelical churches are in such a mess. It has become popular to preach a painless Christianity and automatic saintliness. It has become a part of our "instant" culture. "Just pour a little water on it, stir mildly, pick up a gospel tract, and you are on your Christian way."

Lo, we are told, this is Bible Christianity. *It is nothing of the sort!* To depend upon that kind of a formula is to experience only the outer fringe, the edge of what Christianity really is. We must be committed to all that it means to believe in the Lord Jesus Christ. There must be a new birth from above; otherwise we are in religious bondage and legalism and delusion—or worse! But when the wonder of regeneration has taken place in our lives, then comes the lifetime of preparation with the guidance of the Holy Spirit.

God has told us that heaven and the glories of the heavenly kingdom are more than humans can ever dream or imagine. It will be neither an exhibition of the commonplace nor a democracy for the spiritually mediocre.

Why should we try to be detractors of God's gracious and rewarding plan of discipleship? God has high plans for all of His redeemed ones. It is inherent in His infinite being that His motives are love and goodness. His plans for us come out of His eternal and creative wisdom and power. Beyond that is His knowledge and regard for the astonishing potential that lies resident in human nature, long asleep in sin but awakened by the Holy Spirit in regeneration.

Yes, God is preparing us by making us disciples of Christ. A disciple is one who is in training. Being a disciple of Christ brings us to the day-by-day realities of such terms as discipline, rebuke, correction, hardship. Those are not pleasant words. To be admonished and instructed, to be punished and reproved, to be trained and corrected—no one chooses these things because they are neither pleasant nor entertaining. But they are in God's plan for our spiritual maturity.

In times of testing and hardship, I have heard Christians cry in their discouragement, "How can I believe that God loves me?" The fact is, God loves us to such a degree that He will use every necessary means to mature us until we reach "unity of the faith" and attain *"unto the measure of the stature of the fulness of Christ"* (Eph. 4:13).

A critic may cringe and charge that God is breaking our spirits, that we will be worth nothing as a result, that we will wear only a sad, hang-dog look for eternity. Oh, no! That is not true. What God plans is to bring us into accord with the wisdom and power and holiness that flow eternally from His throne.

God's loving motive is to bring us into total harmony with Himself so that moral power and holy usefulness become ours in this world and in the world to come.

This has been a message from my heart about down-to-earth preparation that will result in readiness for heaven's joys. Let me therefore conclude with a simple, down-to-earth illustration—the example of a newborn baby brought suddenly into the confusion of our noisy world.

Is the little fellow "ready" for this world in which he must live? When the time of his birth neared, the doctor told the parents-to-be, "The baby is ready!" So, as the baby was born, it could have been said in the biological sense that he was "ready."

But what do you really think? You must know that the baby is not really ready at all! From the first little whack he gets to make him cry and get his breath right on for the next eighteen or twenty years, that baby and child and young man will need to learn much about his environment. He will need to mature day by day.

In the broader social and human sense, he is not ready for this world until years have passed and he has completed his formal education. So it is with the Christian believer who has confessed his or her faith in Jesus Christ. Oh, yes, he or she is forgiven and "saved." But is he, is she automatically prepared for heaven and all of the eternal glories above?

To say yes is to be ridiculous. You might as well say that you can pick up a newborn baby, prop him up in the chair of the nation's President or Prime Minister and whisper in his ear that he is ready to govern.

My mind returns frequently to some of the old Christian saints who often prayed in their faith, "O God, we know this world is only a dressing room for the heaven to come!" They were very close to the truth in their vision of what God has planned for His children.

In summary: Down here the orchestra merely rehearses; over there we will give the concert. Here, we ready our garments of righteousness; over there we will wear them at the wedding of the Lamb.